Praise for *The Lies We Tell Ourselves*

"With a blast of truth, Frederickson—a world-class psychotherapy teacher—lays out the essentials of effective therapy. With clarity, a brilliant writing style, and many real-life examples, he shows us how a connection to the truth breaks down the walls and barriers that keep us from having a loving connection with others. *The Lies We Tell Ourselves* is destined to be a classic enjoyed by sensitive people (and their therapists) for generations to come."

—Thomas M Brod, MD, Distinguished Fellow, American Psychiatric Association, and Associate Clinical Professor of Psychiatry, David Geffen School of Medicine, University of California, Los Angeles

"In *The Lies We Tell Ourselves*, master clinician Jon Frederickson affords us a front-row seat to witness the dramatic changes that can take place when we have the courage to let go of our defenses, embrace our true feelings, and step into our lives in a more honest way. You're sure to be inspired."

—Ronald J. Frederick, PhD, psychologist and author of *Living Like You Mean It*

"*The Lies We Tell Ourselves* explodes our illusions so we might come into true, authentic relationship with ourselves and others, the essence of love. The world is full of distortion and avoidance, but Jon creates a startling space where emotional truth can be fearlessly spoken. His writing has the feel of both psychological and spiritual mastery. His brilliant, richly informed, hard-fought, and gritty wisdom is a gift to us all."

—Susan Warshow, MSW, DEFT Institute

T0026321

"In his latest book, *The Lies We Tell Ourselves*, Jon Frederickson shows us how we can face the truth of our lives so we can live fully engaged with the world and not with our fantasies of how we would like things to be. Basing his work on common struggles that each of us face, he shows us how to wrestle with and not avoid the existential issues that are inherently human and that derive from consciousness, such as death anxiety, loneliness, fear of abandonment, and isolation."

—Jeffrey J. Magnavita, PhD, ABPP, Past President, Division of Psychotherapy, American Psychological Association

"Simply reading the loving wisdom in this masterful book by Jon Frederickson is perfect preparation for everyone who is contemplating psychotherapy or who wishes to re-engage therapy at a new level. Mental health and caregiving professionals will also benefit.

"The vignettes in this book take us straight into the sacred space of Jon's rooms where we can fully appreciate the smooth, loving, dextrous, surprising, and profoundly transformative ways in which he accompanies clients through the tragedies of life—loss, separation, divorce, grief, suicide, addiction—into authentic wholeness and fulfillment.

"I wholeheartedly recommend this book to everyone who wants to see what therapy is really about or who wants to increase the value of the psychotherapy they engage in or offer to others.

—Peter Fenner, PhD, author of *Radiant Mind* and *Natural Awakening*

The Lies We Tell Ourselves

How to Face the Truth, Accept Yourself,
and Create a Better Life

Jon Frederickson

SEVEN LEAVES PRESS

Seven Leaves Press
P.O. Box 341
Kensington, MD 20895-0341
www.sevenleavespress.com

Ordering Information

Quantity sales. Special discounts are available on quantity purchases by corporations, associations, and others. For details, contact the "Special Sales Department" at the address above.

Orders by US trade bookstores and wholesalers. Please contact BCH: (800) 431-1579 or visit www.bookch.com for details.

Printed in the United States of America

Cataloging-in-Publication

Frederickson, Jon, author.
    The lies we tell ourselves : how to face the truth,
  accept yourself, and create a better life / Jon
  Frederickson. -- First edition.
      pages cm
      Includes bibliographical references.
      LCCN 2016907072
      ISBN 978-0-9883788-8-9 (pbk.)
      ISBN 978-0-9883788-9-6 (ebook)

    1. Self-deception. 2. Denial (Psychology)
  3. Self-acceptance. 4. Self-actualization (Psychology)
  I. Title.

BF697.5.S426F74 2017
158.1   QBI16-900063

First Edition
26 25 24 23   10 9 8

Contents

Preface

Life is hard, but psychological suffering can be unbearable. To find a way to bear it, we may seek a therapist. A good therapist has an innate wisdom born from the pain of life, a wisdom that can be earned no other way. But once we find such a person, how do we work together to stop our suffering?

To answer this question, we must understand why we suffer and how we return to health. We become ill because of the lies we swallowed and the lies we tell ourselves to avoid pain. Perhaps we swallowed a lie that we are bad rather than recognize that a person wronged us. We might tell ourselves a lie such as "Things will get better" rather than face a crumbling marriage. We become well by facing the truths of our inner life and outer life together. All of us tell ourselves lies to avoid pain: it's human. The problem? We don't see the ways we fool ourselves. That's why we seek a therapist: to help us face what we avoid.

This book can help you see not only the falsehoods that cause our suffering but how to face the truth to become free. It will help you see what therapy looks like when it leads to change. Therapy is not merely a chat, a checklist review, or the "solving" of you as a crossword puzzle. Therapy is a relationship between two people devoted to facing the deepest truths of our lives so we can be healed.

We will explore the lies that make us ill so we can embrace the truth that makes us well. In this era of managed care, we are in danger of losing sight of the soul of therapy. Who are we? Why do we suffer? What are we seeking? This book will try to answer these questions, not through definitions but through vignettes that show how facing what we avoid leads to genuine change.

In these vignettes, all identifying information has either been deleted or changed to protect the confidentiality of the people involved. These stories are used to show the truths we all struggle to face and the universal ways we avoid those truths. In a sense, these stories about other people are about us. All of us struggle to face the truth.

Many of the people presented here have experienced such horrendous pain that you may find their words hard to read. Your task will be to empathize with *their* pain and to recognize *your* pain through theirs. And through these stories you will see how the seemingly obvious cause for our pain is usually not the actual cause of our suffering.

We suffer because we run from life, death, and the teachings they offer. We become healed when we embrace our inner life, our loved ones, and life itself. Is the mystery of you knowable? No, but you are embraceable. This book will show how to embrace the truth of you.

Introduction

A woman sat down in my office, sighed, and said, "I don't know what to do about my marriage. My husband keeps having affairs. We've been in couples therapy, but it hasn't done any good. He feels guilty, or at least that's what he says. But every time he promises to be faithful, he gets involved with another woman. I should leave, but it's easier to stay in the marriage than to divorce."

"He promises to be faithful but then gets involved with other women?" I replied.

"Yes."

"Would it be fair to say that you stay with the man who promises and try to forget the man who has affairs?"

"But I can't forget!"

"You can't forget the facts, but it sounds like you have been marrying his promises."

"That's harsh!"

"It's not my intent to be harsh. Have your husband's affairs been harsh to your wish for faithfulness?"

"Yes."

"And if you believe his words instead of his deeds, will believing his words be hard on you?"

"I see what you mean."

"If I see you hurting yourself, ignoring a behavior you need to see, do I have your permission to point that out so we can bring your suffering to an end?"

"When you put it that way, it makes sense. But we don't sleep together anymore."

"I understand you don't sleep with *him* anymore. But since you are still with him," I paused, "is it possible you are living with his *lies*?"

Her eyes filled with tears. "How do I leave him?"

"You don't need to. The *faithful* husband already left. Would you like me to help you stop waiting for him to come back?"

This woman hoped her faith would make her husband faithful, but it didn't. Why did she lie to herself? Why do *all of us* lie to ourselves? It's easier to embrace our wish than what is here. As the woman's therapist, I wouldn't find out in this session why she embraced her husband's lies. And I might not find out why in the next session either, since meanings unfold over time.

No matter how much we learn about someone, that person will always be a mystery. So if a person is a mystery, psychotherapy is a mystery meeting a mystery.

Why do we go to therapists? With the decline of traditional religions, we increasingly turn to healers to get help, end our suffering, and find meaning in life. Therapy for many has become a secular confessional. While wanting to change internally, we ask others to help us avoid change by validating us, fixing us, or advising us on how to change others. Therapists, drawn by a calling to heal, may correct our logic, listen while we say what comes to mind, or offer insights, but while each of these is an essential ingredient in therapy, none by itself is therapy.

A therapeutic relationship cannot be merely a method, a technique, or an act done *to* us. To heal we must be devoted to discovering the truths we avoid. And we avoid them through the lies we tell each other and ourselves. We don't need advice. We need to delve underneath the lies to find what we have been looking for.

We don't need to be fixed. We may think we need to fix ourselves, but often we are trying to fix our fantasies instead, the broken illusions, shattered self-images, and distorted ideas creating our suffering. Only by letting go of the false can we experience the real. Then we can accept ourselves and rediscover the vitality we lost through our lies.

A wise therapist does not simply talk about our thinking. Therapy is not a head-to-head relationship. A wise therapist does not sit silently while we prattle on, engage in chitchat, or say what comes to mind no matter what. If saying what came to mind mended people, saloons would long ago have healed humanity. A wise therapist does not rely on insight alone, for an insight from the head will not heal the pain in our hearts. How does healing happen?

The therapist invites us to experience who we are under the words, the excuses, and the explanations. We embrace our inner life (our urges, thoughts, and feelings) and the outer world, hidden from us by the lies we have believed about others and ourselves. And by facing what we have been hiding from, we go through the inner challenge known as healing.

If knowledge is the food of the soul, as Plato claimed, then healing happens when we bear what we avoid so knowledge can arise. Pills, shots, and electroshock are not substitutes for the living relationship that therapy can be. This book shows how facing what we avoid can heal us. The examples drawn from my practice present people struggling with the problems everyone has, using the excuses everyone uses, and demonstrate how, together with the therapist, people can bear the unbearable to face what they formerly feared.

Through a series of vignettes we will explore this encounter between two people where a patient heals through a heart-to-heart meeting with a therapist. Although patients may ask for advice and repeat clichés, they long for who they are buried beneath their suffering. What is the knowledge they seek? These days when the concept of truth is often discarded, why do people keep seeking the truth in this embrace known as psychotherapy?

◆

CHAPTER 1

Something Is Wrong

All of us have experienced and been flooded by the pain of life. Overwhelmed by the truth, we avoid it through lies we tell ourselves, lies we don't even recognize, lies we never intend to tell. Sadly, these lies, which may have initially saved our lives, over time become our worst enemies, causing more suffering.

We seek help, thinking we are wrong when our lies are wrong. We wonder if we are broken when our lies are breaking, allowing our feelings to emerge. Running away from our feelings, we tell ourselves more lies that create more suffering.

What if what is "wrong" in us points to what is right? What if we need to stop running and turn around to embrace what we have feared? Facing the truths of our lives not only sheds light on what causes our suffering but also gives us the strength to face those truths.

In this section, we will see how the therapist helps us look at what our symptoms point to: the pain that is too much to bear alone. By looking under the lies and finding the feelings and truths underneath, we return to who we are and what is real.

Therapy as Journey or the End of Journeying?

When we avoid what we need to face, we suffer the symptoms that bring us to therapy. We can bear the pain of life, but our psychological suffering can be unbearable. Perhaps we lost a dream, a loved one, or even the hope that we could be loved. Sigmund Freud called psychotherapy a "cure through love,"[1] a phrase that has generated commentary as vast and varied as the human heart. Yet at a recent conference a speaker referred to therapy not as love but as a technology for change. Has therapy become a technique? What about the relationship? Are we people or objects to be manipulated?

In an era when suffering is reduced to chemicals in the brain, wrong thoughts, or bad genes, the heart calls out to us. We are not buckets to be filled with medications but people who yearn to connect to our inner life, other people, and life itself. We reach out not for a pill to avoid reality but for a hand to hold as we face reality.

Healing takes place between two people who learn by living together and are linked by their mutual struggles when facing the facts of life, loss, and death. None of us are wizards with all the answers. Both patient and therapist are always learning to live and bear the questions of life.

For instance, when I applied to train as a therapist, the analyst who interviewed me asked if I had been in therapy. I answered, "Yes."

"Why did you enter therapy?"

"I was a mess."

I didn't need a technique but a person to help me face the pain of my life. As a child, I had endured too much to bear alone. Lost in my suffering as an adult, blind to its cause, I needed a guide to take my hand, enter the dark forest of the unknown, and sit with me while I sat with myself. By doing so, I could let go of the defenses causing my suffering and sense the wisdom in myself that I had sought in others.

I started what I thought was the journey of psychotherapy. But if it's a journey, where do we go? We go nowhere. In fact, we *stop* going. We stop running from this moment. We can spend an entire lifetime running from ourselves to an obscure objective called cure, recovery, or enlightenment. Yet we need not seek anything because our feelings, our anxiety, the lies we tell ourselves, even the truths we avoid—everything is here.

A woman worried about her forty-year-old son who had autism, became ill, and had to live with her for several weeks until he returned to his group home. She said, "I was so angry with him. He crossed the street without looking and was almost hit by a bus! I yelled at him, 'I need you to be normal! I need you to be healthy!'"

"You need your autistic son to be normal."

"Yes."

"You need him to be *not him*."

"He's got to change."

"A son whose autism has not changed in forty years has to change. Is that true?"

"No. I guess not."

"We wish our anger could un-autism him, but it doesn't, does it?"

"No, it doesn't."

"He keeps being autistic. You have been waiting forty years for a normal son to appear instead of the autistic son you have. I understand. Who wouldn't? Shall we hold the funeral for the normal son you never had and never will?"

She bent over and sobbed.

The reason I reminded the mother of what she had been denying was not to cause her pain but to bring her relief, relief from an illusion that had tortured her for forty years. By facing the facts of her life with her, I showed her that she could face them too. As she let go of her unreal son, she embraced the real son she had.

Can she learn to see things as they are? Can she let her son be autistic? Notice that the truth can be neither given nor received. The therapist can only point toward the truth that is present within the patient. Insight does not come from the therapist's lips but from the patient's heart.

Once the mother acknowledged her wish, she saw what she could now live with: her son as he was. The absence of her fantasy became the space in which her son appeared. When she saw that what she wanted was not real, how to live with her real son became self-evident. Interestingly, the more she faced the truth, the less she suffered from her lie.

Her ability to have fantasies did not die. She merely woke up from the dream her fantasies created. Unable to free her from her wish, I could only help her see that the real son she resisted existed anyway. And her nonautistic son never existed, except in her dreams. In letting go, she surrendered her attachment to the wish for a normal son. The wish would arise again, but she could observe rather than cling to it and return to loving the son she had.

We wait for what is not present rather than be present to what is. Once this woman was present to her son and woke up from her wish, she could say, "My God! I am you. *I* need to become normal. *I* need to look both ways when the bus of reality rushes toward me."

We become well by relating to what is here; we become ill by relating to our fantasies. The therapist stops us from running away from ourselves so we can rest in reality. Remaining in this moment, we feel our feelings, which always reach out to us through anxiety. Anxiety, strangely enough, invites us to dive inside to the places from which we always run, the places we are afraid to descend into and explore.

In effect, therapists always give the same message: "What you run from is where you need to rest. What you fear you need to face. What you ignore you need to hear."

But we have learned not to listen. We live a life on the run, never realizing we are running away from our feelings and what provokes them. We never learn to experience the difference between who we are and how we try to seem. To stop running, we need a partner to help us sit, bear, and feel. For what was unbearable when alone becomes bearable when shared.

This bearing and sharing is not a technique but the mutual embrace of our inner and outer lives: what is happening. And what is this sharing and listening but love? Once this woman embraced her son's autism, she was able to love him, no longer asking him to be what he could never be: the nonautistic child. To heal, together we must embrace the formerly unbearable: reality and our feelings about it.

The Unbearable

"Jon, Jon!" my sister screamed. Two and a half years old, she stood in the baby crib by the window where my one-and-a-half-year-old brother, caught in the curtain cords, was strangling to death. I jumped out of bed, ran to the crib, climbed in, and tried to help her hold him up while his legs flailed. Squirming and kicking, he was too heavy. We kept trying and trying to lift him up to get his neck out of the cords, but we couldn't. I raced to the kitchen to get help. The baby-sitter screamed out the window over the sink to my mom out back, "Florene!" My next memory is of my mother frantically giving my brother mouth-to-mouth resuscitation. Minutes later, as he lay dead on the brown rag rug with a green oxygen tank next to him, a neighbor took me by the hand to her house until after the funeral. I never saw him again.

Life. Death. Guilt over my brother's death. Five years old, I already faced questions I could not fathom.

Yet I am not alone. All those who seek healing had to bear a pain that they couldn't bear by themselves. One patient's mother attempted to drown her. A man's father beat him so brutally that his back and buttocks were striped black and blue. Another woman's psychotic mother stripped her clothes off in the middle of an intersection and, standing naked, preached to the passing cars. Our brothers, our sisters, in pain.

Everyone who needs healing has a story of heartbreak, loss, and feelings so painful that we can't finish our journey. To finish this journey, we seek a person to help us go the rest of the way.

Healing

In therapy we discover that we heal through relating, for the wounds that occurred in relationships must be healed *in* a relationship, a relationship where the therapist doesn't talk *at* us but *with* us. She wants to find out who we are underneath the words, ideas, and fantasies. When she asks for our feelings, not our beliefs, she invites us to a different relationship, another world. She doesn't tell us to shut up, get over it, or forget it but becomes the doorway of acceptance through which our feelings may enter. The therapist reveals to us the depths we feared and supports us while we bear them.

Rather than chat about the outer world, she asks about our *inner* world, the feelings, urges, and desires we have dismissed. She points out the ways we hide from others and especially how we hide from ourselves. Then she encourages us to come out of hiding. "You are the most important person you will ever meet," she says. "Why not be on good terms with yourself?"

To be on good terms with ourselves, we must learn to listen to who we are under the words, the excuses, and the explanations we use. In the next example, a woman began her therapy not by telling me her problem but by describing her trip to the hairdresser and dermatologist.

I asked, "If we leave your dermatologist to the side, what is the problem you would like me to help you with?"

"My former therapist said I was traumatized as a child."

"And you? What do *you* want to work on?"

"There are so many things. It's hard to pick one."

"If you are specific, what do you want me to help you with?"

"Let me tell you about my childhood, and maybe that will help you."

"Before we go to your history, what is the problem?"

She sighed and confessed, "I'm not comfortable getting into that yet."

"You want my help but are not comfortable telling me your problem. If we don't know the problem, what will happen?"

"I won't get help."

"Could this pattern of wanting help and not letting yourself get it be a problem you would like me to help you with?"

Her lips quivered, her eyes brimming with tears.

The therapist has no interest in a patient's facade of being in control because this partial version of herself that she passes off as the whole is the wall hiding the real person she is afraid to be. As the therapist points out the ways the patient hides, and she sees them too, she finally stops hiding. Naked without her defenses, she cannot pretend she is "fine," her facade having fallen.

The therapist welcomes us as we are. One human meets another. The therapist embraces our thoughts, feelings, and anxiety, and we experience what we want and fear: being loved as we are. Although in fact, we never fear being loved. We fear the pain and grief that arise when love's presence reveals its previous absence.

Our world of self-rejection and fear dissolves in this *mutual* embrace of our feelings. Why mutual? If the therapist accepts us as we are but we don't, we perpetuate our secret self-rejection. Healing occurs only when we embrace ourselves too. This embrace starts with embracing our problem.

My patient's reluctance to reveal her problem turned out to be a gift. Her fear of revealing her problem pointed to her fear of depending on me; it revealed her rejected longing for an embrace. Her depression said no to the life she was living, pointing to the yes she was afraid to be. I accepted the resistance she feared I would reject. In this mutual acceptance, the grief flows as a lie dissolves: the lie that we are not lovable.

Is Something Wrong with Me?

We often tell ourselves, "Something is wrong with me." Let's take a look at an example to see what that lie hides. A recovering cocaine addict, who heard voices telling her to use drugs, said, "I don't know what it is, but something doesn't feel right. I don't know what right is, but this isn't right." Sometimes a sense of "wrongness" is a clue to what is trying to grow from within.

This woman had punished herself for years, believing she deserved only to suffer. Why? To support her drug habit, she started to work as a prostitute. Not wanting her daughters to see this, she left them with their father, a former boyfriend. While on the streets, she learned that he had sexually abused their older daughter. She promptly took the girls back and filed charges, but the damage was done. She had chosen drugs over her daughters' safety.

Her previous therapists tried to remove her guilt, urging self-forgiveness, and she feared the same from me. "What I done was wrong! And ain't no one goin' to argue me out of it."

"You're right: you were wrong. You will feel this guilt until the day you die. No one can take away your guilt. And I have no right to try because this guilt is the healthiest part of you. Precisely because you love your daughters, you feel guilt. It's a sign of your love. Therapy can't do anything about that. But we can help you with this horrific self-punishment you have been inflicting upon yourself ever since. After all, your self-punishment does not help your daughter, does it?"

She suffered because she believed a lie about herself: "I deserve to suffer forever." What she thought was wrong with her was right, for her guilt pointed to her love. And when she finally embraced and bore her guilt, she felt her love for her daughters, her inner beauty. No longer needing to punish herself, she stopped abusing drugs and never went back to prostitution. Able to face the damage she had done, she began to work in a day-care center with children, symbolically repairing the damage she had done in the past.

She had been a prostitute. Could pretending to like a career that you don't like be a form of prostitution? A man, groomed for the family firm, became morose after working in the business. "I don't feel right," he said. "I shouldn't be depressed." In fact, his depression was right. Why? He was a skilled painter. His symptoms were tidings from his inner life: leave the business and become an artist. He was depressed because he was living a lie. Once he left his lie and lived his truth, his depression disappeared.

Another woman didn't need to leave her career but to leave a lie she told herself. She asked, "Why am I anxious? My life is great. My children are grown. It makes no sense." Anxiety never makes sense until we face the facts and put them together.

She led the family business while her husband was perceived as the leader. When she set limits with staff, he often undermined her. When we explored her feelings toward him for sabotaging her, she reassured me, "I'm not angry," saying that she believed her anger was unspiritual. She denied that she was angry with her husband, but she blew up with the rest of her staff instead.

Her anxiety pointed to her anger, signaling her intent to become more honest with herself, her husband, and me. Anxiety is a sign of the unspoken. Soon she let go of her facade and set limits with him, asserting her leadership openly without hiding her capacity, what she had hidden for thirty years.

Perhaps this belief that something is wrong with ourselves means that we want to give birth to a more authentic life.

I'm Okay, but Something Is Wrong with You!

At times we say, "Something is wrong with me." At other times we assert, "Something is wrong with you!" We find fault with what is. "My wife shouldn't be late." "My husband *should* know what I want." We start "shoulding" on others. If they aren't the way we want them to be, we think they are wrong. Maybe other people aren't wrong but are midwives who pull us out of our womb of illusion. Could they be helping us give birth to ourselves?

A man outraged over his wife's affair roared, "She betrayed me. She was unfaithful. I can't believe she did this! This is horrible."

It was horrible, but it was also a reality check. His wife's behavior woke him up from his dream that his marriage was fine. Although horrified by her affair, he began to see his careerism as his own furtive affair, his obsession with his job as a brush-off of her. As his marital mirage dissolved, he discovered how his dismissiveness killed her love.

"I told her to buy whatever she wanted," he snapped. "I even put a million into a charity account so that we could run it together. What did she want? I'm a busy man. I'm working up in Manhattan four days a week. I don't have time for all this at-home-dinner stuff. I bought that mansion over on P Street. I figured that would keep her busy."

This man did not love his wife. He loved *how he wanted her to be*. The first days after he learned of her affair, this man fumed in a constant state of outrage. "I told her she had to stop or we were over. She told me to stop yelling at her. I wasn't yelling; I told her I'd cut her off unless she dumped that son of a bitch."

He was shocked because his denial kept bumping into reality. Instead of his fantasy wife, his real wife kept turning up. Why would she object to his wish to control her? It seemed obvious to him—she should obey. For him, only one mind and desire existed. He could not understand why she wanted to abandon his castle. He did not realize that she felt not like a princess, but a prisoner. The moment we are stunned, we can either let the truth in or keep it out with our lies. In this man's case, he sneered, "She's just a selfish bitch. She never loved me. She only cares about herself. I kept trying to tell her what was wrong, but she wouldn't listen."

For him, his beliefs were profound insights. He assumed she didn't love him. His assumption, supposedly true, separated him from the facts. She longed for his love, but he loved his stories more than his wife.

These beliefs, called "projections," seem true because they are real: they are the realities we reject in ourselves and relocate in others. If we criticize ourselves, we imagine others criticize us. If we ignore ourselves, we imagine others ignore us. If we fail to care for ourselves, we believe people don't care for us. However, the persons we project upon can be the mirrors we look at to see, learn, and accept what we reject in ourselves.

From within our playpen, some people appear to be "wrong." We judge them, condemn them, and, mystified, claim we can't fathom them at all. Why? Because they don't conform to our stories about how we believe they *should* be: they should be like us, wanting what we want, doing what we do, and thinking how we think. We want people to be perfect, meaning perfect clones.

Was the wife selfish in her adultery, or was the husband selfish in his self-absorption? Was she a bitch, or was he a bastard? He never loved her. He loved the person *he wanted her to be*, the image he tried to bully her into becoming: the "right" version, according to him.

The phrase "You are wrong" really means, "I am frightened of the truth you evoke in me." As a colleague said, "The truth will heal you, but first it will hurt like hell." No wonder we accuse other people of having our faults.

Unable to face the truths in himself, this husband kept attributing his selfishness, his lack of love, and his betrayal to his wife. When we take back our accusations, we feel the pain of self-recognition.

What if "wrong" people are deported aspects of ourselves waiting to be reunited with us? What if the wife's love affair echoed the husband's affair with work? Later, after his wife apologized for the affair, he continued to judge and condemn her; he was blind to her effort to reach out to him. Does his wish to judge rather than listen reveal that he loves judgment instead of her? If so, shouldn't she seek love elsewhere?

Even as she apologized, he continued judging her vulnerability, the vulnerability in himself that he detested and that the affair exposed. Imagine if we could say, "Oh supposedly 'wrong' person, thank you for permitting me to meet myself in you. I hate in you what I reject in myself." Instead, we push our flaws away onto others.

When therapists invite us to admit that we attribute our own flaws to others, we bear the pain of self-recognition. But when we peer into our mirror—the "wrong" person—and embrace him, that moment of embrace becomes a homecoming. The feelings "wrong" people stir up within us are the feelings we imagined were in them. We can continue to see others as "wrong" and refuse to face what is within us. Or we can allow people to return us to ourselves.

I Feel Broken

Coming home to reality sounds good but not when reality means losing a job, being fired, falling ill, getting divorced, or dying. In response to hardship, we often believe we are broken, crushed, or ruined. What breaks? What is crushed? What is ruined? Our illusions break. Our hopes are crushed. Our dreams are ruined. We look out the window and the world seems the same. We look within ourselves and see our shattered fantasies.

The breakdown of our fantasies can allow the truth to break through. We believe we are broken, blindsided by life, yet we are still here. So did we break, or did our self-image break? Did we die, or did our dreams die? How hard it is to watch our cocoon of illusions collapse.

Consider, for example, a man who denied the severity of his wife's mental illness. He kept hoping for a normal wife who would accept help instead of his psychotic wife who rejected dozens of treatments. As his illusion tottered and before it crashed to the ground, he tried to push it back up: "Do you think she might benefit from body therapy?" he asked, allowing denial to triumph over experience. Thinking he was loyal to her, in fact, he had been loyal to his wish. His tears broke through, revealing his underlying reunion with the real.

As the author Jeff Foster says, "Breakdown can always point to the break-through of a deeper truth, since only that which is false in you can break down. Truth does not break. Some call this recognition 'waking up,' some call it 'self-realization.'"[2]

A woman hallucinated that her bedroom was moving. To make it stop, she banged her head against the wall. She cried; her hands were bloody from having clawed them. Her husband had left her. The world had moved, and she couldn't stop it. She redirected the rage toward the husband she loved onto her head and hands.

"I feel broken," she said. "I can't kill myself, because I have to stay alive for my daughter, Lora, but if she weren't here, I would. I'm broken into pieces." She imagined *she* was broken when her *illusions* were broken. She saw the walls moving, but life had moved, as it always does. Her fantasy that life stays the same—denial—crashed into reality, so her denial began to dissolve.

When facts kill our wishes, a few of us may seek to kill ourselves to wipe out the pain of the dying wish, what the suicide researcher Edwin Shneidman called "psychache."[3] Experiencing the living death of the dying dream, we may choose physical death to abort the painful birth known as grieving.

This woman believed she was dying, becoming more broken. But her illusions were collapsing, allowing for the possibility of what was really there to appear. We never break, although we imagine we are breaking. Our illusions break, and all our denial and all our demands cannot put our fantasies together again. And when our denial breaks, the grief and rage start to flow. In this outpouring, the fire of feelings doesn't burn us; it burns up our illusions.

Since we fear the loss of our illusions, we tell our friends stories about how we were wronged. These stories seem true because they are internally consistent, but they are actually false because of what they exclude: the rest of reality. The beauty of distortion is that by dismissing enough information, we can demonize anyone and turn a person into a cartoon, while treating a story like a fact.

Nothing like divorce triggers this urge to demonize. A man who had bullied his wife was enraged when she left him after several years of marital therapy. This woman, although flawed, had also been patient, loving, and devoted. Once she left him, he converted her through his imagination into a liar, a cheat, and a coward. He complained to anyone who listened, offering a well-honed litany of her flaws. Omitting many of her strengths, he described a virtuous woman who mysteriously turned into a witch. "Now I know who she really is. No one sees what I see. People see her good side, not the real her. She's so good at hiding it!" He called his friends, and recounted her imaginary crimes: "There's something you need to know."

When we, delighting in demonizing our "oppressors," parade a cartoon figure before friends or therapists, they can indulge us by joining our pity party, a masochistic fiesta[4] where we sing our songs of victimhood, bemoaning how life happened differently from our fantasies.

This man waited for his "victimizing" wife to change and thereby victimized himself. He imprisoned the only person he could change: himself. We believe that we are victims because we do not see how we victimize ourselves. Instead we blame others for what we do to ourselves, becoming blind to the real culprit.

The man who bullied his wife insisted that *she* had been a liar, a cheat, and a coward. Yet by acting as if he could bully her into becoming a clone, *he* lied to himself and to her. Further, by bullying her, he made love to an ideal image and thus rejected and cheated on his real wife. Bullying is always the mark of a coward, a person who so fears life that, rather than embrace it, he tries to bully it out of existence. When the husband's illusion was broken, he tried to break his wife, so she broke out of his bubble.

The therapist must question our song of victimhood. Rather than concur with our caricatures, he invites us to embrace the facts we cast aside. When we face the facts instead of fixate on the fictions, we accept that our loved ones have good and bad traits just as we do. *We* have been victimizers too. Others hurt us and we have hurt others. We are tempted to claim that we are innocent victims, yet we are never faultless, blameless, or guiltless.

Embracing life on its own terms can be difficult. As we embrace life as it is, our illusions collapse. We need emotional courage to bear the pain without running, explaining, or justifying. In victimhood, we ask others to agree with our stories. We must drop the stories to see who we are underneath.

As we let go of our facades, we feel naked. As I helped one man face what he had avoided, he accused me: "You are trying to expose me!" I explained, "The good news is that I can't. Only you can expose yourself. I can ask questions, and you can expose yourself or not. The choice is yours: do *you* want to expose yourself to yourself so you're no longer going through life blind?"

When he chose to expose his inner life, he discovered that we are always naked. Our facades are imaginary and invisible. We try to hide who we are, but others see us anyway. We can never be apart from reality except through the veil of our illusions. Without facades between us, we realize on the deepest levels that each of us struggles with feelings, lies, and longings.

What If Feelings Are Forms of Love?

What do we learn in therapy? The truth. How do we learn? By embracing it. Who is our teacher? This moment. To make sure we notice the truth, life sends us messages: anxiety, anger, sadness, depression, good and bad relationships: whatever is happening. When we have trouble embracing what life brings, we reach out for help. Or we procrastinate.

One young woman waited for the life she had to turn into the one she wanted. Angry because her boss refused to give her a promotion, she asked, "Do I have to accept this?"

"No. Life will wait until you are ready."

"I don't feel ready yet."

"How long would you like to wait?"

Waiting is the magic wand we hope will make life fit our fantasy, but our fantasies must change to fit what is here.

When we stop waiting for life to change, we change instead. Every crisis in life cracks our defenses and unlocks our feelings, revealing hidden dimensions in ourselves. And after bearing those hidden dimensions, we experience insights rising from within. When we dive inside, we experience ourselves more deeply and find the wisdom for which we longed. Then we can choose whether to deny or embrace it.

This choice doesn't happen once in a lifetime but in every moment. In one session, I saw a man's tears, so I asked, "What are you feeling now?"

"I'm thinking of the time—"

"But now?"

"Yesterday I—"

"But the feeling?"

He burst into tears. "I remember when my father was dying, and everyone assumed he couldn't hear us, so they didn't talk to him. I sat next to him and told him about the party we had just attended. As I was talking to him, he reached out and patted me on the shoulder." Suddenly he realized that the father he hated had loved him.

His new insight came from his depths. Feelings reach up inside us that we fear will pull us down, and they will; they pull us into our depths, the source of all knowing. By descending into his grief, he experienced not only his father's love *but also his own love* for his father, the gift that he was for his father.

Bearing our emotions transforms us into a prism. As we refract the spectrum of feelings passing through us, a special form of light appears, the light known as insight.[5] The man's insight about his father came not from his head but from his heart.

After we surrender our denial, our illusions fall off and the feelings rush in, allowing the person we are, whom we have yet to meet, to emerge. Feelings are forms of love, invitations to embrace what is, so the false can drop, revealing the real in you.

What Does Our Suffering Point Toward?

If every feeling is a form of love, what about feelings resulting from trauma? Imagine being flooded with anxiety. How could that be love?

A man was captured and tortured by terrorists who raped and killed his wife in front of him. Somehow he escaped, fled from his country, and became a refugee in a faraway land. Overwhelmed with multiple symptoms, he sought help.

Doctors tried many treatments and drugs to heal him from the effects of the traumas he suffered. Nothing helped until a therapist repeatedly asked what the anxiety pointed toward: "What feelings are causing this anxiety?" The refugee's emotions continued to rise until the secret crossed his trembling lips.

After the horrible rape and murder of his wife, he escaped. But before he left his country, he had one more thing to do. Obsessed with revenge, this man who had been the hunted turned himself into a hunter. He found the killer, knocked him out, bound him, and skinned him alive.

The refugee's anxiety pointed toward the trauma he suffered and the one he inflicted. By torturing the torturer, he became what he most hated. In turn, he was tortured by anxiety, guilt, and self-punishment—the price exacted by revenge.

Revenge is a form of magic. When we exact revenge, we pretend that we can get rid of our pain by putting it in other people. The husband did not pry the sorrow from his heart by pulling off the skin of the killer. Instead, he abdicated his humanity, which he skinned off himself that day.

Because he tortured the killer, he had to bear the guilt for the torture he inflicted and the pain, grief, and helplessness of watching his wife suffer. By confiding his crime to a therapist, he faced his guilt over the acts of murder and torture *he* committed. He faced his grief—which he had tried to avoid through revenge—and, finally, reclaimed his humanity.

He hoped to rip the pain out of his own heart by ripping the skin off the killer. Like him, when we suffer from pain within ourselves, we might try to get rid of it by inflicting it on others. Yet try as we might to bypass the pain of life, we cannot. By definition, life always includes us: our grief, our rage, our guilt, and our illusions. Our suffering points toward the truths we fear to embrace inside ourselves.

◆

CHAPTER 2

How We Avoid the Truth of Our Lives

Why do we tell ourselves lies? To avoid the feelings that arise when we face and embrace reality.

We often avoid the truths of our lives by waiting for fantasies to become true rather than face what is true. Waiting for what is real to become unreal is how we lie to ourselves about our loved ones, ourselves, and life itself. We suffer because we fight reality, a fight we always lose.

The lies we tell ourselves are invisible to us. That's why we need a therapist to help us see those lies and the costs they inflict. Then we can begin to face the truths we avoided.

When we let go of the imaginary, we face the real. And by embracing our feelings and reality as they are, we not only discover who we are, but the world as it is, so we can begin to walk into it and the truths it reveals.

Suffering

The horrors of the tortured man and his raped and murdered wife are gruesome. Not all stories are so appalling, but this does not mean they are less moving or painful. Each story shows how therapy can free us from the illusions misguiding our lives, and invite reality, the trustworthy guide.

Illness reveals good health as a gift we will lose. When death "steals" our lives, it points out what we possess: nothing. Our bodies, our minds, our lives, and our loved ones appear to be ours until the last gasp exposes our ownership as a mirage. The losses of life can peel away our illusions, revealing that all is given and nothing is owned.

Loss is neither right nor wrong. Life is as it is prior to our opinions. We believe life should show up on our terms, but it shows up on life's terms instead. Surprised to discover that the world is not made in our image, we judge death for interfering with our fantasies of life without loss. But no matter how much we fight reality, reality always wins.[1]

However, the losses of illness and death don't always necessarily peel away our illusions about life. From the mindset of denial, death is unfair and unjust. Rather than face what is, we may choose what is not here, waiting for our fantasies to appear and make reality disappear. When we maintain our illusions, the life we have passes by while we wait for a fantasy life that never arrives. Thus, the losses of life are compounded by the losses we inflict upon ourselves.

Death is part of reality. We might face the death of a person, a marriage, a relationship, a career, or a dream. All our desires give birth to a death, for every desire for what is not here is fated to die when it meets the world, when the yearning for permanence meets impermanence, and when the wish for the infinite meets a limit.

A woman longed for her brother's love even though he had rejected her, screamed at her, and stolen her inheritance. Unable to find his love for her, she sought it through his daughter, whom she visited and cared for. Then one day her brother told her she could no longer visit. Deprived of her last hope for a loving bond with him, the dam broke, the grief flowed, and her denial floated away.

Did she feel better after grieving the death of her fantasy? (She still had a relationship with her brother, just not the one she wanted.) "I have never cried like I did last session. It was so painful, but I feel relieved," she said.

I asked, "What do you make of that?"

"After I cried I realized I could face the truth. I didn't realize until I was crying how hard I had tried to avoid it. I knew it, but I hadn't really faced it until last session. I don't have to fight it anymore. I feel lighter."

We get attached to fantasies of how we should be loved, respected, or desired. Our suffering is not caused by these fantasies but by our *attachment* to them. This woman was attached to her wish for a loving brother who didn't exist. Face-to-face with a dying wish, we can either grieve as this woman did, or we can mistakenly claim life is worthless when, in fact, our self-image is. This woman realized that her love for her niece was meaningful, but her story of being a beloved sister was not. She had to grieve the losses she suffered and the ones she inflicted on herself through refusing to embrace her brother as he was.

Reality often disappoints whereas fantasy seduces us with the promise of infinite fulfillment. When we see a therapist, we mourn the deaths of those seductive promises. When we avoid these painful feelings, we suffer the symptoms that result from ignoring the emotional truths of our lives. In therapy, we can face the feelings we have avoided and stop living in a world that no longer exists.

We go to a therapist to face the facts of life and the feelings they trigger; we hope therapy will make our suffering go away. And it can, but when facing the loss of our illusions, we may choose the secret protest: resignation.

Me: "I give up fighting, but I still hate you."

Reality: "Take your time. No rush. You can despise me as long as you want. People can spend an entire lifetime doing so."

Me: "You are not fair."

Reality: "Fair is the name you give your fantasy. You are surprised when I show up instead. You imagine your hatred will change me and undo the loss of your dreams. It's too late. I already shattered your illusions. When you are ready, we can hold the funeral for the dead self-image lying in the coffin."

What a difficult funeral to hold when we cling to a treasured self-image of one who is loved, victorious, admired, or right. These self-images are the conceptual clothes that hide who we are. Life pulls them out of our hands and we cry, but we have one more strategy for clinging to our self-image: we can treat sadness as a problem to work through and get over.

Grieving

Our grief is not a problem, however, but a path. When we grieve, we surrender to the truth that washes away the false and leaves behind the real. We do not get over grief but live through it in a communion with what is. In this communion, we need not give up our illusions since the tears wash away our attachment to the fantasies that ward off life.

As an example of the healing power of grief, a self-destructive man who had never met a bridge he couldn't burn came into therapy when his world had collapsed. Facing a lifetime of self-sabotage in which he had destroyed every major relationship, he said, "I need to get past this shame and guilt."

"What if they are the paths to healing? Shame is a sign from deep within that you did not live up to who you wanted to be."

"That's true," he said tearfully.

"This guilt over the people you hurt points to your love, the higher part of yourself asking you to come home."

"I don't think I ever tried to live up to my better self."

"You don't need to get past the shame or guilt. You need to go through them. They are signs of who you are, the man underneath the facade of detachment."

His guilt and shame did not cause his suffering; his lies did. We are never hurt by our deepest feelings, only by our resistance to them. Embracing life as it is, we bear intense pain. We believe we are dying when our fantasies are dying, removing the veils between the facts and ourselves. And at last we can rest in the truth of who we are.

In a later session this man grieved the ways he had destroyed earlier relationships. He saw that he had been a "phony" in life whom no one could rightly love. While sobbing over his losses and bearing the guilt over his lies, he said, "I can never thank you enough for giving me back my humanity." In fact, I couldn't *give* it back to him since it had always been within him, hidden under his lies.

The Universal Addiction

The degree of our suffering equals our distance from reality. Rather than end our suffering by running toward the truth, we run farther away from it through food, work, alcohol, drugs, and sex. Mistakenly considered addictions, they merely point to the true addiction. We are addicted to not being here. We don't want to feel what we're feeling. We don't want the present but the imaginary past or future.

The man I described earlier who killed the murderer who killed his wife did not want to feel what he felt or remember what he remembered, but those feelings and memories were true. Killing his wife's murderer could not unmurder his wife.

We are hooked on an imaginary experience of the not-me, not-now: the universal addiction. Food, drugs, Internet, sex, fame, work, and booze are tools we use to leave the real world for an imaginary world of how we think people *ought* to be. We long for an idealized past or future, which never existed. We can't live yesterday today. Rather than be present to what *is* present, we wait for what we *wish* was present.

We imagine that if we lived in a different time or place, we would find our inner home of calm, rest, and contentment. Craving the not-me, not-here, and not-now keeps us homeless. We try to escape from this moment by racing to the next, but this moment is the only home we ever have.

We race toward another time, place, or way of being in hopes of completing ourselves, when we are already complete. Without realizing it, while running toward what we want, we leave who we are. What *would* complete us is the embrace of everything we feel now, but we do not want what is here. We want what we wish, seeking the wish we prefer rather than embrace how we are. We shop for the fantasy we want, believing that what we want is faraway, when what we need to know is here.

We try to run from, fend off, and stop what we don't like, racing from our fear, the beacon. Fear is a light that directs us where to dive: into our resistance. When we embrace what we fear in ourselves, the marriage between the inner self and outer self is consummated.

Often, however, rather than realize we are resisting feelings in ourselves, we resist the people who trigger our feelings. For instance, we resist our spouses, ignoring what they say and waiting for them to say what we want them to say. This separation from who they are, however, can lead to a divorce in our marriage. A middle-aged man wearing a baseball cap, cutoffs, and sandals sat down in my office and told me in a detached voice that his wife wanted a divorce. After years of struggle, individual therapies, and couples therapy, she had given up on the marriage, but he still wanted to try.

"I can't believe she wants a divorce," he said.

"You don't have to believe it for her to believe it."

"I don't see why she wants a divorce."

"You don't have to see why she wants a divorce for her to want one."

He smiled. "Yeah, I know, but it doesn't make sense."

"It doesn't need to make sense to you for it to make sense to her."

"I don't want to give up."

"It may not be time to give up."

"Yes, I want this to work out."

"Can we accept that you want this when she doesn't?"

A hint of sadness flickered across his face. He admitted, "We took a trip with the kids recently and it was nice," he paused, "for a day." He paused even longer and smiled. "Until we had a fight, and she said, 'You are angry with me, aren't you?' And I said, 'I despise you.'"

After this crack in his denial, he said, "You probably think I'm in denial, but I don't want to give up."

If I pointed out his denial, I would only reinforce his belief, but he would be no closer to seeing his own denial. I decided to play back his denial, thinking if he saw his denial in me, he would more easily see it in himself.

"Why give up? Maybe next week, next month, or next year will be the right time. Maybe it's important to hold on."

Sighing, he admitted, "Yeah. I mean there's the kids and she hasn't thought through how it's going to work."

"Given that you have kids, she hasn't thought this through, and she asked you to move out in November; maybe you should not give up now."

The smile faded from his face, and he sighed. "Several years ago she no longer wanted sex with me. She said we could stay together, but no more sex, and that's really important to me."

"Although she doesn't want sex with you anymore, and she wants a divorce, maybe you should hang on."

"When we were first together, she was so sweet and caring."

"What a loss! Why leave the sweet girl who cared for and loved you?" His face reddened as he looked away, tears trickling down his cheeks, leaking through his denial.

The separation caused his pain, and denial caused his suffering. He denied that his wife felt what she felt, thereby damaging his marriage. Rather than listen to his wife, he listened to his wish. No wonder she asked for a divorce: he had divorced her feelings and words and married his denial. Did his intercourse with denial lead her to stop sexual intercourse with him? He waited for a divorcing wife to turn into a loving one, but by waiting for his wish, he forced his real wife out the door. Punishing her for failing to be his fantasy, he used guilt to bully her into becoming the woman he wanted. She left him because he had already left her for the image in his mind.

When he denied that his wife wanted what she wanted, I could have argued with him, but the conflict would have appeared to be between him and me. When I mirrored his denial, he experienced the conflict between his denial and reality. As a result his pain leaked through. He closed his eyes, but his wife's wish for divorce did not disappear merely because he didn't see it.

The only way she might reconsider divorcing him was if he stopped divorcing her feelings and words. She had no reason to listen to him if he listened to his denial instead of her. He could end his suffering by relating to her rather than waiting for her to become another person. He did not realize that his relation to an ideal image of his wife was an imaginary relationship.

He denied reality to avoid his feelings about it. The price? Ignoring his wife's wish for a divorce did not stop her from divorcing him.

Running Away: The Geographical Cure

We rarely run away from problems outside us; we run away from the feelings in our hearts. Not realizing that we fear what's inside us, we mistakenly fear what's outside us. We try to run away from our problems: the geographical cure, but we cannot lift ourselves out of life. No matter where we go, our shadow follows: our feelings. Everything we run away from inside us always reaches out for our love. Yet rather than reach out to what reaches out to us, we race away, refusing to sit in, rest in, and be transformed by our feelings.

Although we call therapy the "talking cure," we can use words to talk away from the feelings we need to face.[2] A young woman talked to me, racing over her feelings. I interrupted and asked if she saw how quickly she was talking.

"I always talk like this," she said.

"You race over your anxiety and feelings. What do you feel if we look underneath the words?"

"But I have so much to say."

"Of course and can we look inside and notice what you are feeling?"

Her face filling with sadness, she said, "I feel nervous."

"What is the feeling underneath making you nervous?"

She began to sob.

Once we stop talking away from our feelings, they rise for our embrace. We imagine we are far from what we need to heal, but we always have the exact experience we need: the one right now, the one we don't want, the one we run from.

In our race to find wholeness, we forget. Trees do not rush to grow. We never pull on a bud to make it blossom. A flower never asks to be different or further along. It bears the inner pressure of life pushing the petals out to form the bloom. Have you ever taken a single rose, one that you find especially beautiful, put it in a vase, and watched several times a day as it aged? It changes but never loses its beauty, even when the last petal lies on the desk next to the vase.

We are more complex than a flower. Feelings reveal who we are, and if we divorce our feelings, we cut ourselves off from our depths. We sense a loss, even if we cannot name it. If we decide instead to sit with the discomfort of our feelings, we can discover who we are under the words, excuses, and explanations. Can we sit with the not knowing and the desiring to know as we blossom?

What will happen if we open up to another person? We can't know how we will blossom, how a relationship will bloom, how life will unfold. Can we bear not knowing who we will become?

To heal we must accept our fear of revealing ourselves to a person we haven't met and our fear of *becoming* who we could be. We come to a therapist to unfold, change, and find out who we are underneath the ideas others fed us, the ideas we believed, the ideas we embody without even realizing it. Not only therapy is unknown. *We* are the uncharted territory never explored, the potential never plumbed.

How can we judge addicts? We are addicted to not bearing what we feel or being who we are. We are stoned on imaginary selves, imaginary others, and imaginary states of mind: the real drugs.

Fortunately for our growth, life shows up instead. Ever faithful, it rises every day to be seen and embraced, triggering feelings and our opposition to what is. Reality invites us to reunite with the external world.

The therapist makes a similar invitation: "Are you willing to face and embrace who you are so you can heal?"

"I don't want to be me. I am addicted to the image I want to become."

"Your addiction is not the problem. Accepting your addiction is the next step toward the wholeness you seek. How you are is what we need to embrace."

"I hoped I could divorce my addiction."

"No. You hoped you could divorce your outer life and inner life, but they are married to you forever."

The Universal Lies in Life and Therapy

To reject our inner life and outer life, we need to lie. But this lie is different, universal, and even invisible to us: it is a defense. As the psychoanalyst Donald Meltzer said, defenses are the lies we tell ourselves to avoid pain.[3]

A woman who was betrayed by an unfaithful husband said, "He shouldn't have done that!" (Lie: reality should not be what reality is.) A man who was physically abused as a child by his father said, "I'm glad my father beat me. I deserved it." (Lie: I pretend that only my love exists and not my rage toward my father.) A woman whose husband had left her said he will come back. (Lie: if I unsay reality, reality will disappear.)

Imagine a woman who distanced herself in relationships, remaining lonely, isolated, and depressed. I asked, "What is the feeling toward your husband for having an affair?" She answered, "I feel empty."

Without realizing it, she lied to herself and to me. Can I relate to an empty woman? Or should I point out how she hides behind her facade of emptiness? Do I believe her lie? Given enough pain, all of us have pretended to be empty when we were *full* of feelings. None of us are in a position to judge others for hiding their feelings.

She emptied herself, inviting me to relate to an empty woman in an empty relationship. In response, whether as friends or as therapists, we must embrace a fact: she lied. She has feelings because we always do. She just hides them from other people. Why?

As children, we hide our inner life to cling to a parent we cannot share the truth with.[4] When we share a feeling, we share the truth of our experience in this moment. If a parent becomes angry or anxious when we express a feeling, we learn to hide our feelings to make a parent less anxious and to preserve our relationship. This woman learned to pretend her feelings had disappeared, acquiring this language of concealment as seamlessly as she did her mother tongue. The problem is that our feelings do not disappear only because we hide them.

This woman's close relationships in the past led to pain. Since her mother had distanced from her, the woman distanced from her own feelings and from me. However, her problem, distancing, is also her gift to us: she shows in the present how others hurt her in the past. In this way, obstacles to love reveal the wounds to be healed.

She expected me to accept the empty relationship with her that she had to accept as a child. But if I accepted her "emptiness," we'd have an empty relationship. Instead of accepting the relationship she offers, which harms her, I offered a relationship that heals.

When she said she felt empty, I responded, "You say you feel empty, inviting me to relate to an empty woman. Then we will have an empty relationship. You put up a wall of emptiness between you and me. What feelings are coming up toward me that make you create this barrier?"

"I'm not sure I want to work with you."

She threatened to leave if I was honest, like her mother threatened her. Hearing her threat, I said, "It sounds like you have a reaction to what I said. What are you feeling toward me?"

When people threaten us when we are honest, we might agree with their lie to avoid a conflict with them. But by embracing a person's lie, we become in conflict with the truth, when the person's lie should be in conflict with reality. If we embrace that lie, we abandon the person.

When I asked what she felt, she said, "I don't think I have a feeling. I mean I could throw out something, but it wouldn't be real."

"Right. You invite me to relate to an imaginary person to have an unreal relationship. This is a barrier you put up between us. What is your feeling toward me that makes you create this wall of the unreal person?"

In therapy we often discover that people were given the message as children, "Lie, and I will love you. Tell the truth, and I will leave you." If not said in words, it is often said in action. In response, the child may sacrifice her integrity, honesty, and even her sanity, for the love of the parent she needs to survive. Many of us go on to live lives that embody that destructive message.

Whether as therapists or friends, we should live the message "Because I care for you, I will be honest. If you shame me, I will not borrow your shame. You accuse me of hurting you, but your lies hurt you. Truth, being the food of the soul, can never damage you, but the falseness that hides who you really are is poisoning your soul."[5]

All of us lie. The moment we invite a person to be close, the age-old question returns: "Can I tell you what others could not bear, or must I hide what I feel?" In the past, we had to live a lie. The therapist invites us to let go of our lies, so we can live the truth together.

Love Addiction or Addiction to Denial?

We try to run away from our feelings, but we can never escape who we are. Nor can we escape from what is happening in this moment, except through imagination. Yet when facing the loss of a past love, an imaginary love can be seductive.

A man sought therapy to let go of his ex-girlfriend. "I know that holding on to her hurts me, but I can't stop waiting for her. I don't want to say goodbye to the chance that she still wants me." He paused and wondered, "Maybe I'm addicted to her."

Yes, he was addicted, not to her but to denial. He could have related to the fact that she left him. Instead, he interacted with his fantasy: "She'll come back." To fend off his feelings due to the breakup, he denied what happened and tried to live in his wish.

The object of his addiction was not his ex-girlfriend. She vanished. He was addicted to his *fantasy*: an imaginary woman who wanted to unsay her words, retrace her steps, and live happily ever after with a man she abandoned.

"I want her back," he said.

"You wish the girl who left would return. Who wouldn't want a rejecting girlfriend to turn into a lover? Why let go of that?"

"I know it's negative if I hang on."

To help him see his illogic, I enacted it so he could see it and hear it outside of himself: "If you hang on to a rejecter, she might turn into an accepter. What's negative about that?"

"I don't want to wait for her. I can't help it."

"You can't help wanting the image in your mind instead of your rejecting girlfriend. It's important to love her while she rejects you. Can we accept that?"

"I don't want to say goodbye to the chance she still wants me."

"You don't want to say goodbye to the chance she will turn into someone else."

"The memories of the good times hurt."

"No. The memories remind you that you are waiting for the woman who left. And waiting for what is gone hurts you."

When she rejected him, he rejected the facts and waited for her to unreject him. If we wait for the universe to do things our way, we had better have ten thousand lifetimes. Standing by the roadside with his thumb out, life was passing him by while he waited for a fantasy that never came. "Reality is painful, but denial is dangerous."[6] If we wait for the life we want, we lose the life we have. By facing the reality of loss, we can grieve what has passed, and embrace what is left.

In the throes of desire, we assume that the facts can be other than they are in this moment. This man was not addicted to love but to a nonexistent girlfriend who would unring the bell, make time rewind, and resume a life of loving bliss. Denial was his drug of choice.

Optimal Hopelessness

As a drug of choice, denial is useless. No matter how much we deny what is happening, it still happens. Why? Denial is a thought. Can a thought know reality? Can a thought replace what is here? Can a thought make a fact disappear? Sometimes it seems worth a try, especially when, for example, a husband uses his wife.

A woman was angry because her husband no longer paid for house expenses nor wore his wedding ring. She told me she wanted to mention the money to him for the thousandth time but felt hopeless.

"That makes sense. Would you agree that bringing it up again *is* hopeless?"

"I can't believe he doesn't pay his share of the expenses."

"That's okay. You don't have to believe it for it to exist."

"I don't get it."

"You don't get reality."

"I keep hoping he will change."

"You keep hoping the reality of your husband will change."

"Shouldn't he want to pay for his children?"

"Shouldn't he be the same as you want him to be?"

"It would be nice."

"Yes, it would. We can wish this were true, but it's not. We can rage at what no longer exists, or we can take another path. Giving up on this road doesn't mean you give up on yourself or on life. It means taking another path."

"I get it. I have to face reality."

To hope that the real will become unreal is not hope but denial. Life bumps into our illusion and reveals that resisting facts is futile. This woman was not hopeless, nor was her husband. Her delusion was. We don't need to give up on a person or on ourselves but on a hopeless *fantasy*. Then our suffering stops. She needed to stop waiting for her husband to turn into her fantasy in order to release herself from her suffering.

We rage, hoping life will turn into our wish. The result is a sore throat. Life still exists as it is. Once we accept that our wish is a fantasy, we rest in optimal hopelessness: we recognize that it is hopeless to wait for what is true to become not true.

When we let go of the imaginary offerings of our illusions, we become open to the real offerings of life. As the philosopher Ernst Bloch points out, genuine hope occurs when we reach out to find what *has* been stretching toward us.[7] When we reach out to the real, we feel hope in the possible. At that moment we seem to expand. Hope does not expand us, however. Hope reveals the expanse that lives outside our fantasies, the inner expanse that we are but had forgotten.

The therapist helps us see the lies that blind us into hopelessness so we can see what is real, pursue it, and regain our hope. The moment we leave the path of denial, the path to the possible opens. We must give up hope in hopeless fantasies to regain realistic hope in what is real.

I Can't Stand It!

Rather than embrace what is and let our illusions dissolve, we ask life to wait until we can "handle" it. For instance, we claim that "this is too much," we are "not ready," or "what happened should not have happened."

An outraged businessman said, "I can't stand it! She knew what she was doing, and it was wrong!" He had ignored his wife and her complaints. Then she had an affair.

We say we can't stand it, but we do. "I can't stand it," means, "I don't want to." Who does?

Life seems to be against us. Yet since we are life, we cannot separate ourselves from it. Life includes us. What is "against life" is our belief that life should be the same as our fantasy.

Our beliefs always lose because life doesn't obey our orders. It may appear that it is too much for us, but it's not. Life is too much for our beliefs, shattering them every day—if we're lucky. As they shatter, we mistakenly think we are falling apart, but our fantasies, masquerading as our essence, are dissolving into nothingness.

And who better to shatter our fantasies than a child not living up to our hopes. A mother had failed to protect her son adequately from an abusive father. Later in life, the son blackmailed the mother into supporting him financially, claiming that *his* problems were *her* fault. He kept browbeating her until she broke down and coughed up more cash. As I showed her how he blackmailed her, the ways she tried to purchase his forgiveness, and how her bid to "buy peace" bought more war, she said, "This is killing me."

"No. This is killing your illusions."

She nodded, pursed her lips, and burst into tears. "But I don't want the relationship to be harmed."

"How can you harm something that no longer exists?"

She related to the imaginary son she wanted, not the real son she had. And she wished he would relate to her, not to the projection he had placed upon her. He viewed her as an evil person who deserved to suffer for eternity and should pay reparations until death. She feared the good relationship she desired would be harmed, but it didn't exist and hadn't existed for decades. He saw an image, not her. She saw an image, not him, for she longed for a loving son, the one who had disappeared.

As we let go of our illusions, we can live the truth we feared. When this woman gave up waiting for the son she wanted, she stopped trying to buy his love, and loved the real son she had instead. The blackmail came to an end.

Before burying our dead hopes, we may stage another protest: "Why does this happen?" Translation: "Why does reality happen to me?" Life whispers, "Why not? I happen to everyone else. It's nothing personal."

Take me, for example. I used to say, "I never get sick." Then I was diagnosed with cancer. My fantasy, previously viewed as a fact, fell into the psychic trash bin. I didn't fall apart; my thought did. Tumors didn't need to fit my mind to grow in my body.

"I don't understand why this is happening," we say. That's okay. Whatever is happening does not need our understanding. It exists whether we understand it or not. Not registering the facts, we try to bargain with the universe, hoping life will say, "You don't get it? Fine. I won't show up until you do."

One way we fight facts is by refusing to understand our spouses and asking them to explain themselves until we do. An irritated wife asked her husband, "Why do you spend so much time playing online chess?"

"I enjoy it."

"It doesn't make sense. It's a waste of time. It's not productive."

"Look. I have done my chores. I have free time. I enjoy this. How do I get you off my back?"

"You have to convince me why it's a good idea."

It was not his job to convince her why he liked what she didn't like. She tried to bully her husband by not understanding him, hoping he would say, "You don't understand me? Okay. I'll stop being me until you understand why I have a right not to be you."

She gave him the message "How can I manipulate you to want what I want? If I can dominate you, my problems are over." This strategy always fails because differences never end. We want the whole person without the parts we don't like, but the parts make the whole.

Our spouses will never shrink to match our understanding nor stretch to fit our fantasies. Why? Reality, being everything, includes our fantasies, whereas fantasies are *designed to exclude* what is real. We fail to realize that we want to change a fact, a fact that continues to exist—for instance, the fact that a husband likes chess. Devoted to our fantasies, we avoid facing what is here.

A woman argued with her deadbeat husband who refused to look for a job. For years, she berated him for his behavior. She even relished a secret pride in "fighting the good fight" for her daughters. What did her fight achieve? She showed her daughters how to stay with a neglectful partner, wait for him to change, complain that he was not changing, and be proud of her choice to suffer: the heroism of masochism.

We ask people and life to change to be the way we want, and they do change. But they change their way, not ours. When they don't change our way, our illusions can dissolve or we can hold on to them more fiercely. If our illusions dissolve, we feel pain.

While bearing the loss of our dreams, we need not be strong. We need only stand still without running while the true burns off the false.[8] Hopes, thoughts, and ideas are so many moths burning up in the flame of life.

We hope to control what is, but we are like a wave trying to shove the river of life. The river is still here after the wave dies on the shore. We try to reject what is, but it cannot reject us. It always embraces us, try as we might to wriggle out. Can we accept reality's embrace and return it?

Resistance = Suffering

When we embrace life, we cannot avoid pain. It is inevitable. We will lose everything we have and everyone we love before or at the moment of death.

In contrast, suffering is optional. Experiencing heartbreak, we may use defenses, the lies we tell ourselves to avoid the pain life brings. But our defenses—the ways we avoid reality—cause more suffering. We push away what is happening and the resulting feelings. "I'm not angry, just disappointed." "I can't believe it!" "She couldn't have meant that." Yet life keeps leaking through.

Remember the hallucinating woman whose husband left her? Facing *his* betrayal and the pain it caused was the easy part. Later in therapy we discovered that for years she had complained about the ways he treated her but then she waited for him to become someone else.

The hard part was facing how she had rejected him for years and blamed him for not being the way she wanted him to be. In fact, she had not been married to him but to the image she wanted him to become. Thus, she had divorced him years before without realizing it. Waiting for him to turn into someone else, she deprived and punished herself, calling it loyalty. She never realized that loyalty to the unreal was betrayal of herself.

At first, she thought he had been cruel to her. Eventually, she realized she had been cruel to him and to herself. Her task was to embrace the facts: he had left her, and she had left him, herself, and her feelings.

Taking responsibility for the life *we created* is hard when playing the victim is so easy: "*They* created my life!" The siren song of victimhood sounds so sweet, pure, and righteous as it lures us out of the river of life. We retreat into a netherworld where others are bad, we are good, and all is perfectly clear. Lost within our fantasies, we forget who we are: the space in which those illusions arise.

In the reassuring certainty of victimhood, we *know* what they did, *why* they did it, and what they *should* have done. All this "knowledge," seemingly simple, true, and obvious, is merely our assumptions, factual only within the fantasy world dreaming between our ears. In fact, we never plumb the depths of another person completely. Since our understanding of others is always incomplete and partial, our "knowledge" is always a lie: a splinter masquerading as the tree.

And the "shoulds" are our directives to the universe. We tell people how they *should* be according to us, but the cosmos never notices; it goes its own way—not ours. Life keeps bumping into our shoulds: our fantasies of how we wish life would be.

When we expect what we want instead of life, we feel victimized by life, unaware of how we create our suffering. A depressed woman, furious with her husband, said he was insensitive, thoughtless, and cruel. I asked for an example. Through her tears she described how her husband had put his fist into her anus during lovemaking, causing excruciating pain. Horrified, I explored what happened and was shocked again: her husband asked permission to insert his fist into her anus during their lovemaking, and she gave her consent.

"He put his fist in my anus, and it hurt," she said.

"He put his fist in your anus. Is that true?"

"Yes. I told you."

"May I offer you a different perspective?"

"Go ahead."

"He asked you whether he could put his fist in your anus, right?"

"Yes."

"You could have said no, but you said yes."

"He didn't want me to say no."

"Right. You said no to yourself instead."

"Oh."

"You told him he could put his fist in your anus. In effect, *you* put his fist in your anus because you told him he could, but you blame him for your choice. You said no to yourself, and you blame him for that choice. Do you see what I mean?"

"I didn't think of it."

"If we think of it that way, what did you feel toward him when he asked to put his fist in your anus?"

"I didn't like the idea."

"But your feeling toward him?"

"I was angry."

"You were angry with him. Then you dealt with your anger by turning it on yourself by inviting him to hurt you."

"I forgot that I was angry with him."

"Right. You felt angry with him, forgot your anger, and turned it on yourself by inviting him to hurt you. It was as if you invited him to punish you for being angry with him."

"And later I invited him to criticize the food I made for dinner."

"Yes. You invited him to punish you again for being angry. Is it possible that the person who is being cruel to you is you?"

She had been convinced *he* was cruel, *he* should be more sensitive, *he* should be more thoughtful. Yet by inviting him to hurt her, she had been cruel, insensitive, and thoughtless toward herself. In this victim stance, she asked him to love her when she refused to love herself. This strategy was doomed to fail because *his* love could never erase *her* self-hatred.

With the collapse of our imaginary victimhood, we see how we victimized ourselves, and the grief flows, revealing who we are.

Instead of giving up on our fantasies, however, we may mistakenly give up on life. A woman in an abusive relationship asked, "Am I supposed to give up on my husband?"

"No, but you may want to give up on your self-punishment."

"Am I supposed to change?"

"It's not a matter of whether you are supposed to change, but whether you want to."

"Supposed to" is a hidden violence, an inner directive to do what we don't want to do, feel what we don't feel, and be who we are not. The best we can do in the moment may be to accept that we want to reject reality and cling to our illusions a little longer.

We can cling to illusions by asking our spouses to change into our favorite fantasies. A woman on her second marriage complained about her husband's habits of watching television, buying DVDs, and spending time on charity work. She admitted that he was a good husband, but she kept trying to convince him that his hobbies were wrong. These arguments had escalated until her husband had threatened divorce, another deed he *should not* have done.

"How can I convince him that he is wrong to spend all his time watching football on the weekends?" she asked.

"Since he likes watching football, why shouldn't he like what he likes?"

"Do you watch football?"

"No. Since he likes football, why shouldn't he like watching it?"

"Because it's a waste of time."

"According to who?"

"Me."

"Right. Since it's a waste of time for you, you shouldn't watch football. Since it's a pleasure for him, he should."

"But I can't stand it!"

"Maybe he's right. If you can't stand him the way he is, you should let him go, so he can find a woman who can love him the way he is."

"I give up!"

"That makes sense. Either you give up your wish for a man who wants what *you* want or you will have to give up your husband. You cannot avoid divorce. Either you divorce your fantasy of sameness or he'll divorce you because I'm willing to bet another woman will love him in spite of his wish to watch football on Sunday."

She wanted to control her husband to make him fit an image in her mind. But we never control reality, which never fits the images in our mind. When we swear off our fantasies, we unite with what is. Until then, the suffering caused by our resistance whispers to us: "You are lost in your fantasies; come home."

Dancing on the Table

Rather than come home to a painful truth, we try to get rid of it. During a dinner years ago, an acquaintance of mine asked her husband, my wife, and me, "What would you ask for if you could have anything in the world?" We thought for a minute and answered. When her turn came, she said, "I have no need to dance on the table since I've been analyzed."

I was puzzled by her comment at first until I realized what she meant. She wasn't playing the game she had started. We revealed our desires; she didn't. Then we learned a troubling truth. She believed psychoanalysis had purified her of neurosis, replacing her old personality. We had desires; she supposedly didn't. I was angry that she had set us up and troubled by her yearning to be purified, thus boring.

She imagined that she needed to get rid of who she was to become who she wanted to be. A soul sister, she was showing me what I wanted from therapy too! Instead, we must let go of who we wish we were to be the presence we are.

Although therapists sometimes view psychotherapy as a modern "technology," the word "psychology" originally meant the study of the soul. Why did her study of the soul turn into her contempt for it? She didn't realize that to heal, we must embrace our inner messes, not eradicate them.

If a man confesses that he has been a petty thief, shall I condemn his conditioning or embrace it and the person underneath? Can I allow a shoplifter to touch and move me? Can I find wishes to steal within myself? What if he is showing me aspects of myself that I fear to face?

Healing occurs when we love our depths no matter how messy and pathological. Remember the joke: what is psychotherapy? It's when a big mess meets a littler mess. Our raw vulnerability to life never goes away. Our task is not to eliminate but to embrace our humanity, often through embracing the humanity of others.

What do I doom within myself when I refuse your humanity? Your flaws are the mirrors in which I see myself. When I look into you, can I embrace your "defects," meaning what I reject in myself? When I do, you and I discover one less dividing line between us. With every yes, we step closer toward embracing the other person's depths, which are, in the end, our own.

Zero Negativity

At a conference a presenter described his goal for marriages: zero negativity—a relationship with no conflicts. I like science fiction too, but conflict is embedded in our lives. We have conflicting desires within ourselves and between each other. We always have different desires because I am not you, and you are not me. That's not a problem, but how we are made.

I told a friend that zero negativity was a fantasy of returning to the womb. He corrected me. Even there we find negativity: the fetus ingests drugs her mother takes, and the mother is exhausted in the act of giving birth. We seek idyllic, nonexistent forms of closeness without conflict.

Do I wish everyone agreed with me? Yes. Does that happen? No. Is that negative? Not to my growth. If I step out of myself and let go of my other-image (my secret demands of others), I learn to accept people as they are. This is the first step toward love.

We long for a world where everyone gets along and the lion and lamb lie down together. What a beautiful story! When life shows up instead, we become angry. "My preference did not happen!"

We want an imaginary world to avoid the real world. We yearn for spouses who want what we want, groups who cooperate, and colleagues who agree. "Don't be who you are. Be who I want you to be." We compare what happens with what we think should be happening and try to escape into our wishes.

Our demand for zero negativity reveals a negative mindset within ourselves. If I want no conflict, I don't want you. Is there room for you *and* me? Is there room in me for the truth of you? If the universe has accepted positivity *and* negativity, why don't we?

I go for a walk. I see the sun, the moon, and the stars. Looking down, I see dog feces on my shoe. In therapy we look inside ourselves and discover a landscape equally inclusive.

We are made messy, but we try to reject any part of reality that does not fit what we want. When we decide what we will accept and dismiss the rest, we sentence parts of ourselves to death row. We try to sanitize ourselves to appear like the purified pictures in our minds. This is not love, but hatred of life. When we try to transcend life, we reject it.

To aim for zero negativity, we must reject the negative in ourselves. A priest confided his self-hatred to me. I asked, "According to your theology, God made you in God's image. Is that right?" He nodded. "And from your point of view, does God love you?" He nodded. "Since God made you in his image and loves you, wouldn't it make sense to join Him by loving yourself?" His eyes filled with tears.

◆

CHAPTER 3

The Refusal to Embrace

Having looked at the reasons we tell ourselves lies, we can examine the ways we deceive ourselves and distort reality. Rather than let go of our lies and face the truths they hide, we often refuse to embrace the truths of our inner and outer lives. We will explore the ways we ignore the parts of reality we don't want to see—how we oppose them, relocate them, or try to change them. Each of these lies causes suffering in its own pernicious way, resulting in different forms of blindness.

A therapist will not collude with our defenses but show us how they cause our suffering. Then we can embrace the truths of our inner life (our feelings, thoughts, and wishes) and our outer life (reality). This task, never easy and always painful, is made bearable when we bear it together.

"You Keep Forcing Me!"

What if the refusal to embrace our outer life reflects the refusal to embrace our inner life? Opposing others may be how we oppose ourselves. What if outer conflict mirrors an internal war?

People may create a conflict with us to avoid a conflict within themselves. For instance, an unemployed man entered my office, sat back in the chair, rested his arms on the armrest, and waited for me to begin. "I notice you are looking at me expectantly," I said.

"You're the therapist. What am I supposed to do?"

"Nothing. What do you *want* to work on for *your* benefit?"

"If I knew the answer, I wouldn't be here. I'm out of a job. I haven't been looking. And my wife is bent out of shape that I stay home playing on the computer."

"I understand your wife is bent out of shape, but what do *you* want me to help you with."

"I don't know. I don't trust myself anymore. I've been in other therapies and nothing worked. I feel like I have to do what you say; otherwise I won't get better."

"If you do what *I* want, you will get better at submitting to people and making yourself miserable."

"My point, exactly! I didn't want to come, but I'm worried about what you will make me do."

"I can't make you do anything. I can ask questions, and you can answer them or not. It sounds like you might make yourself do therapy when you don't want to."

"I have to force myself because it would be good for me. You would say I won't make progress unless I do this."

"You distrust your no to therapy and try to submit to me."

"I view your invitation as a forcing function where you coerce me."

"I can't coerce you to do what you don't want; only *you* can coerce yourself. Is this a pattern, making yourself do what you don't want?"

"Yes, all the time."

"Is it hard to listen to your no?"

"I don't trust anything I say."

"That's not true. You trust your reasons for submitting, but not your no. You distrust yourself and try to trust me instead."

"Yes, that's true."

"You don't listen to your no. That's important because a no to me can be a yes to you. You say yes to others but no to yourself."

"That's right."

"But in therapy you would only get better at submitting. The therapy would make you worse!"

"That's why I told my wife I didn't want therapy."

"You shouldn't submit to therapy because that would be slavery, not therapy."

"Funny you say that. I was a slave in my last job, and I have said no ever since."

"I doubt you said no to work but to the slavery you imagined work would be. Since you submitted, you didn't know how to avoid turning work into slavery, like here."

"I hadn't thought of that."

"Would you like me to help you stop submitting and saying yes to what you don't want?"

If we cannot say no to others, we cannot say yes to ourselves. We submit to others and blame them for our choice, unaware that we abandon ourselves. To embrace our desires, we must hear our no to others, the inner yes to ourselves, especially when we don't understand our no.

Psychosyrupy

Not only patients but also therapists can refuse to embrace the facts. Years ago at the Washington School of Psychiatry, a wonderful colleague, Morris Parloff, suffered from an allergy, not to pollen but to misplaced empathy. Suppose a man describes a phone call in which he didn't listen to his wife and mocked her as "ridiculous" until she slammed down the phone. When the man rages because she hung up on him, the therapist says, "That must have been hard for you." Morris called this kind of response "psychosyrupy," a form of pseudoempathy.

As therapists or friends, we should empathize with the person, not the behaviors that destroy his life. If we support how he dismisses his wife, we collude with his blaming and denial and help him damage his marriage. He will not see how he rejects and *creates* the wife who hangs up the phone. Pseudoempathy for the defenses encourages self-destruction rather than empathizes with the man who is destroying his marriage.

He may think we are empathic if we agree with his victim stance, but, in fact, we perpetuate his suffering. If we care for him, we are honest even when he becomes angry, for then he knows we back him, not his self-sabotage.

When we are honest, he may say, "You're not listening to me!" In response, we say, in effect, "No, I am listening to you, not to your lie. When you ignore how you dismiss and blow off your wife, you are lying to yourself. If I listen to your lie, I would not be listening to you. I'd be abandoning you. I know this hurts, but I wouldn't say this to you unless I knew you could face it." We don't converse with the lie but with the person hidden underneath it.

Saying the truth frees him from his lie. If we empathize with his lie, we leave him trapped within it. When I described to a businessman how he was destroying his marriage, he became angry with me and claimed, "You are attacking me."

"I'm not attacking you. I'm describing your behavior. Did I attack you, or does blaming and dismissing your wife attack you and your marriage?"

"I thought you cared, but you don't."

"Should I support you or the destructive habit killing your relationship? Do I have your permission to point out when you hurt yourself, or do you want me to sit silently, watching you destroy your marriage?"

He threatened to leave unless I abandoned him: "If you keep talking about this, I'll quit!"

"Okay. I can't stop you from quitting if you don't want to hear what I say. If what I say is not true, you should leave. If it is true, it will stay true whether you leave or not because the truth is always with us and cannot be left. I could lie to you like others do, but is that really the relationship you want? Why deprive yourself of the healing you longed for?"

From our depths we long for honesty even if we ask for a lie. Psychosyrupy covers lies with pseudoempathy; psychotherapy uncovers what is under the lies. Knowledge is the food of the soul;[1] lies are the poison. Whether in therapy or in our closest relationships, our lies heal no one, no matter how much syrup we pour on top. When others tell us the truth, they remind us of who we are, whom we had forgotten, and whom we want to find.

Return of the Rejected Self

We also avoid facing ourselves by attributing the truths of our lives to other people. We attribute our desires to them and wait for them to act on these wishes, which we deny as our own. For instance, a man entered his therapy session saying, "I don't know what to work on."

"Okay," I replied. I waited.

Fidgeting in his chair, he blurted out, "What do you think I should work on?"

"I don't know."

"But you must have an idea."

"No."

"Why not?"

"You came, right?" I asked.

"Yes."

"And obviously you wouldn't come here for no reason."

"Yes, but I don't know what to work on."

"So a man without a psychological problem comes to a psychotherapist's office."

He squirmed in his chair, sighed, and admitted, "Well, my wife wants a divorce. I suppose you think I should look at that."

"Only you can know if you should look at your divorce."

With a heavy sigh, he said, "If I don't, she'll leave, and I don't want that."

Until we perceive the desires in our hearts, we see them in the hearts of others. This man did not relate to me. He interacted with his wish, which he relocated in me. Then he opposed or distanced himself from *my* wish for his therapy.

As long as he warded off his feelings by wishing them away into me, he could never feel, face, or see what was in himself. Since he thought that *I* wanted him to work in therapy, he could not see what *he* wanted to work on. Rather than face the desire within himself, he examined the one he imagined in me.

For a while, this strategy works: other people appear to have our feelings and desires. Then life happens. A loved one leaves us, a boss criticizes our work, or a child gives us a dose of snark, and the feelings we reject rush back in with a vengeance. Why?

The feelings we reject travel temporarily to other people *but only in our imagination*. In fact, they live within ourselves.

We can project our inner life onto other people or onto objects. For instance, one man saw eyes in the bushes and trees gazing upon him wherever he walked. The hallucinated eyes satisfied his wish to be seen and known by a remote mother who abandoned him during his first year of life. So much longing and heartbreak was located in the branches above him.

Whenever we reject our feelings, we send them away through projection, asking them to live in other people. When life happens or we are near those we project upon, we feel the feelings we believed were in those people. It's as if our feelings migrate home after living in other humans.

The man who said he didn't know what to work on was anxious. He wondered what I wanted from him, never realizing that he was reacting to his desire, which *he imagined* was in me. My presence roused his disavowed wish within himself. He thought I *made* him feel when my presence *triggered* his feelings and desires, the missing pieces, that were trying to make him whole again.

In fact, no one can return our feelings to us since those feelings never leave; their "travel" is only in our imagination. After we stop fantasizing about imaginary feelings and desires in people, we accept the feelings that we believed were outside but that were actually inside, within ourselves.

Life triggers our disavowed feelings, and anxiety is its messenger. Anxiety is the sound of those feelings knocking on our heart's door: a sad child, an angry kid, or a hopeless one asking, "Can I come in? Will you love me?"

Instead, we reject the feelings arising within and send them to another person. Perhaps it's a spouse, a child, a friend, or a boss, but we must find somebody to be angry, limited, selfish, or critical: we don't want to recognize those qualities within ourselves. Having banished our feelings into other people, we distance ourselves from them, analyze them, judge them, and even punish them.

How do we identify the qualities we deny in ourselves and attribute to others? Our judgments, complaints, and habitual beliefs about people are the mirrors in which we can look to see ourselves. The traits we judge in others we reject within ourselves. We complain that others hurt us to avoid facing how we hurt ourselves. We ignore within ourselves what we focus on in others.

What if we get married so we can blame spouses for our problems? A married man invited me to conduct a telepathic therapy with his absent wife: "My wife has a problem with intimacy," he said.

"Do you notice you invite me to relate to her problems instead of yours?"

"She has issues."

"That may be, but do you notice you invite me to pay attention to her and not you?"

"Yes."

"When you invite me to pay attention to her, you ask me to ignore you."

"Oh, I didn't mean to do that."

"That's important. When you invite me to ignore you, we have a problem with intimacy between you and me."

Examining our complaints gives us the chance to see where the blame belongs: in us. Rather than admit what we have done, however, and study our complaints to discover our inner life, we project our problems onto others. Then we lose sight of what's inside us by imagining what's inside them.

The therapist helps our warded-off feelings return home or, more accurately, helps us face the feelings that never left home because they always lived in us. Projections we thought were "not us" were ours all along. We reject our feelings, desires, and urges and imagine we can send them away to live in other people. What if our feelings, longings, and impulses were never bad? Our feelings reach out to give us the information we need.

By rejecting our feelings, we reject ourselves. We project those feelings onto other people. *They* are angry; *they* are selfish; *they* are critical. And we stay away from them or try to control them, never realizing we are trying to control the emotions we pretend are in them.

The destructiveness we see in others is in us. They do not need to be fixed. We should love them rather than try to fix them; doing so will also fix what's inside us.

Our spouses and others and life itself trigger the feelings we try to avoid within ourselves. We deny those feelings and urges, sending them away, but no matter how far we throw away our feelings, they keep coming back. When we say, "He makes me feel . . . ," we mean, "He reminds me of what I tried to get rid of in myself."

Outside the window, tree branches, a blue sky, flowers, and clouds appear. The universe accepts everything. Likewise, everything human is within us: thoughts, feelings, and urges. We try through imagination to send what is inside outside. Then we sense a longing, a longing for what we refused to embrace: the abandoned parts of ourselves.

Can we open our hearts to other people, the abandonarium[2] of our rejected feelings, and let the feelings come home, where they have always resided, inside us? When we do, we experience the space we are, the space that holds our inner life.

What Can I Do When I Can Do Nothing?

What better place to put our feelings than in our family members? Where else should we make impossible demands? And why pick anywhere else to fight, when we have so much practice doing it there? Often, "family" conflicts are conflicts with reality.

For instance, a woman we discussed earlier had a conflict with her fifty-year-old son. The father had sexually abused the son as a child. As soon as the mother found out, she sought help, arranging therapy for her son and the family. Sadly, the son did not benefit from therapy; instead, he developed and then nurtured a conviction that his mother had destroyed his life and, further, that she should support him financially, a belief he had bullied her with for thirty years. "My suffering is your fault, and if you don't support me, I'll kill myself," he said. The mother was vulnerable to this threat because she not only felt guilty for the son's abuse but for her sister's suicide in her youth.

"He said if I don't pay, he'll report me to the licensing board, and I'll lose my ability to practice law."

"Which would not work," I said. "He threatens you, as if you should pay for eternity." She cried, "I failed him." I agreed, "Yes, you failed him for a period in childhood, and then you did what you could to the best of your ability. Right?" She recounted how she arranged therapy, admitted her mistakes to him, arranged special tutoring, and put him through college until he dropped out. "He says that his father's abuse destroyed his life and it's my fault."

"Your ex-husband's abuse traumatized your son. And the way the two of you handled things created problems. That is your responsibility, but for the past thirty years he has made his mistakes, created his misery, and sabotaged his ambitions, career, and marriages. You didn't do that. He did. You are responsible for whatever mess you created until he was twenty, but he is responsible for the messes he created the past thirty years and the messes he creates today."

"I thought if I paid for private schools for the grandkids that he would help them, but he lets them skip school, not do homework, and watch television."

"You thought you could buy their future, but he threw their future and your money down the toilet."

"I feel like I have to defend myself."

"No. You are trying to defend a self-image. You loved this image of the perfect mother and gave money to your son, hoping he would restore it, but this wish is a secret vampire that sucks the life out of you. Once you drop this image, what is there to defend? You failed him once as a child. Okay. No need to defend that. It's true. He must make his life; you can't do it for him. That's true. Your actions in the past make it harder for him today."

"He says I'm trying to buy his forgiveness."

"And after two hundred thousand dollars over thirty years the evidence is in. You wished your payoffs would buy his forgiveness. They didn't. He discovered that refusing to forgive you pays very well."

She burst into laughter, paused, and said, "I tried to tell him he is ruining his children but he doesn't listen. He either screams at me on the phone or hangs up. I know he'll call back because he needs money. He has to face reality."

"No he doesn't. He hasn't faced reality for thirty years: he was fired from every job, ruined every relationship, and has been unemployed, refusing to look for work, claiming you should support him in the lifestyle he has become accustomed to. It looks like you have been nominated to be the person who looks at reality."

"That is true."

"I can understand that you wish he would face the facts first, but that makes you the hostage of his craziness."

"I can't wait any longer. I can't afford it, but what if he gets enraged with me?"

"He won't be enraged with you. He is enraged with the facts of life. Once you stop putting your money between him and the facts, he can be enraged with reality as a first step in engaging and facing it."

Our loved ones can make terrible choices, and we can't always stop them. Rather than bear the grief inside us, we try to change them to make our pain go away. When we try to change them by sharing insights with them, we provoke rage at worst or perplexity at best. We think we are putting out their fire when we are trying to put out our own, the fire of pain, rage, and loss. We never extinguish a fire in ourselves by pouring our fire on others. The kindest gift we can offer our loved ones is to own our projections and follow the advice we keep giving them.

It is hard to sit in our feelings, so we export them onto others. We try to coerce people into being who we want them to be through explanations, instructions, or demands. The latent message remains the same: "My perception should be your reality!"

Wilting under our wants, people may do what we desire, making us happy when they cave in to our demands. When they don't, we judge them, tell them they are wrong, and, without their consent, appoint ourselves as their much-needed advisors. Then we are surprised when they are less than delighted by our guidance.

They react with rage because we reject them the way they are. We treat them like home renovation projects in constant need of improvement. We give them the message, "You are *almost* good enough for me, but first you need to change."

Other people are not here to become lovable to us, to reject themselves the way we reject them. We are here to love them the way they are, to surrender to what is true: they should be who they are, not how we want them to be. And that surrender might mean that we have to love ourselves when they can't. Then we set limits. This doesn't mean we ask them to change their behavior, which we can't control. We change our behavior, no longer rewarding them when they harm us or our relationship. We face reality while loving them, no longer collaborating with their destructiveness.

This is easier said than done, especially when our hopes are burning in a fire our loved ones set, blow on, and maintain, even if they blame us for setting it and ask us to put it out. The mother had to accept that her son was an arsonist who set his own life on fire, and neither her love nor money would put out his fires when he kept setting new ones.

When loved ones disappoint us, we can let go of the image they didn't live up to, bear our feelings, and allow life to be revealed as a mysterious gift. Or we can ward off our feelings, cling to our illusions, rebuff the relationship we have, try to buy the one we want, and call these actions "love."

What if the mother's disappointment in her son is not a problem but an opportunity? Continual disappointments do not reflect upon others but upon us; they reflect our resistance to what is happening. If you disappoint me once, that is information about you. If you disappoint me dozens of times, that is information about me: my denial of reality. We can't be repeatedly disappointed unless we keep denying what is true, only to be surprised by its return. By disappointing our wishes, people help us see what is here.

When we embrace our disappointments rather than deny them, we can grieve, letting go of our hopes and fantasies of a family renovation project. To face what is, we must bury our illusions in the boneyard. The mother did not die that day in my office. Her hopeless hopes did. We performed the last rites for the son who used to love her.

She fantasized that money could purchase her son's love and health, but she could not buy back the life he threw away. Through his actions, he sent her a perverse love note: "Give up. *Your* love cannot stop *my* self-destruction." Constant disappointments crucified her fantasies on the cross of reality.

When she said, "I can't take it!" I reminded her, "You already did. You've taken it for thirty years, but your denial can't take it, and it is breaking under the strain." We think we are in charge of what is happening, but life is in charge, and it dissolves the fairy tale of existence being our way instead of the way it is.

We try to push life up to the mountaintop of fantasy, but life rushes back down to the lower world of reality. Life teaches us, and one of its finest instructors is our family. Remember the story of the three little pigs that lived in houses of straw, sticks, and bricks?

Whatever is happening challenges the house of *thoughts* we live in. Devoted to our growth, our family reminds us of what is. Life continues to huff and puff, and we keep clinging to the walls of wishing that already blew down.

When we stop clinging to our fantasies, we can begin to accept and love the family we have, and discover the mystery they are, people whom we thought we knew but really are only coming to know. And even if our family is rotten or evil, loving means we will not deny the truth, and we will let their evil teach us what we need to learn.

When the mother let go of the son she wanted, she started loving the son she had. No longer able to bully his mother, her son had to face the fact that he had no choice but to have a better relationship with her. Why? She no longer joined him in his old destructive dance.

Pushing or Embracing?

When death blows down our dreams, how do we listen? A therapist told me about a woman dying of cancer. The patient's surgeon nicked a tumor while removing it, spreading cancer cells throughout the patient's body and leaving her with a fatal prognosis. The therapist told her supervisor, "I'm afraid pushing her for her feelings will be too much for her." Her supervisor agreed, "This is a deep intuitive truth." The supervisor's support left the therapist feeling validated yet troubled, so she raised the question with me: "Do you think her feelings will be too much for her?"

"It's not possible to push her," I said. "Cancer and death did that. Have you noticed how cancer and death never knock on the door to ask if they're too much for us? Life comes whether we are ready or not, but it's not that we aren't ready: our illusions aren't."

"How do I know whether she can take it?" she asked.

"She already took cancer and death."

"I see what you mean."

"It's not too much for her. She is still here." I paused. "Is it too much for you?" I waited. She looked at the floor.

"She is dying. You can't save her. She is enraged with a doctor whose failure killed her. She is losing the life she hoped for—the chance to grow old, to see her children become adults. Will you hold her hand, face her death, and bear these feelings with her?"

"It's painful."

"That's true."

"You are challenging me."

"No. Life did that. In fact, life is not challenging you. Life is challenging an image of therapy. You thought your supervisor validated you, but she validated an image of therapy and life with sunlight but no darkness, skies but no clouds, and possession but no loss."

"I felt she supported me."

"She supported your wish to run. And all of us want to run from death rather than learn from it. I'm a great runner from life myself, but if you wanted to abandon her, you wouldn't have brought this up. Because you know this, you won't let go of her hand when she's in her deepest need."

"It's painful to watch her die, and I can't do anything."

"You can't make her pain go away. You can't give her life, but by acknowledging her pain, loss, and death, you make it more bearable because the two of you are facing it together."

"That wasn't the job description at social services."

"Therapy isn't a job, an occupation, or a profession. It's a calling. Her cancer, her dying, and her suffering are calling out to you.

Now you must answer her call, listen to the hand by your side that wants to reach out to hers, and sit beside her while she dies."

"This is so uncomfortable!"

"Of course. We feel pain too as our dreams for her and the therapy burn up. We can't save her. Everything goes up in flames, but eventually the fire dies down, and in the ashes, you and she will discover what is left, something you can't know yet, put into words, or describe. She'll discover who she is under the words, dreams, and illusions, and so will you."

We try to push life and death out of ourselves, but they continually embrace us, pushing out the lies. As friends, healers, or therapists, we must embrace death as well—the death of our relationships, our hopes, and our dreams. As we sit with a dying person, we realize we are dying too. By embracing what is, both of us learn who we are under the words in the quiet stillness.

Psychological Cherry-Picking

Rather than face what is, we pick the parts of life that fit our fantasy, reject the rest, and try to live outside reality. We think we are running from the outer world, but we are running from what the outer world evokes: the inner world—our feelings and anxiety. And we never escape from who we are.

The feelings that choose us guide us. Through grief, we face loss and feel love for those who died. When people ignore our boundaries, anger helps us defend ourselves. Fear is not a danger but a signal, alerting us to dangers, internal or external. Thus, feelings are positive, promoting our survival.

Why, then, do we judge feelings as negative? We reject them: "I don't want to feel this way." As psychological cherry pickers, we call feelings we want "positive" and feelings we don't want "negative." We try to split the world in two, hoping to live in one half and leave the other. We think we should be all good, but we keep being how we are: good and bad.

Since bearing all we feel within ourselves is painful, we try to avoid one half of ourselves. A man who meditated for decades avoided his anger, believing it thwarted his spiritual growth. He claimed, "Anger is unspiritual. Whatever you pay attention to grows, so you should never be angry." He used meditation techniques to zone out, trying to purify himself of unspiritual feelings. However, skirting his anger turned him into an exploding doormat who appeared passive until he threw tantrums at work.

The psychologist John Welwood has called rage avoidance "spiritual bypassing."[3] We can, and often do, misuse spirituality to sidestep feelings, conflicts, and life. Longing for states of detachment—mislabeled as transcendence—we achieve a form of spiritual divorce. This man tried to transcend his inner life by rejecting it and burying his emotions, not realizing he had planted a seed that would grow from within.

He treated experiences he didn't want as nonspiritual garbage. Yet just as the air cannot leave the wind, we cannot leave who we are. Feelings and thoughts arise within us *and always will*. We never escape who we are because we are neither an object nor a location.

Rather than bear our inner life, we try to slice it off. This is not therapy or spiritual practice but psychic self-amputation. As the philosopher Simone Weil reminds us, "Life does not need to mutilate itself to be pure."[4] Yet people mutilate themselves, mistaking a body part for a hated part of their humanity; they hope to recover their purity through self-cutting.

The very idea of purity divorces us from what is true because life includes purity *and* impurity. By trying to purify himself spiritually, this man attempted to separate himself from his feelings and life to live in an alternate world where anger did not exist.

His self-image, how he thought he *ought* to be, contradicted the facts: who he was. We push ourselves to become the idealized picture we cherish. This never works because we are reality. The picture of what we *should* be is fantasy.

If we give up the violence of self-purification, does awareness ever have a problem with whatever arises? Does a mirror reject whatever appears?

Life is not a supermarket where we shop for feelings to put in the cart and leave the discards on the shelf. Why split life in half and discard the rest? In therapy we embrace everything and in the end, we don't even need to embrace our being since we have always been what we are.

Hunting

Rather than embrace life and ourselves, we engage in cherry-picking or its opposite. One man seized on the most negative facts of his life, turning them over in his mind repeatedly until he suffered from chronic rumination. Obsessed with the worst, he could not see how he created a partial view of the universe or that his negative view, not the universe, caused his suffering. He mistook his rumination, a cherished habit, for a higher form of thought. To counter this, I noted that when we see dog feces on the sidewalk, we manage to walk by rather than pick it up, sniff it, and put it in our pocket. Startled, he stared at me and asked, "Oh, you mean I'm a turd hunter?"

I Have No Blind Spots!

When no longer searching for turds, we hunt for a better truth elsewhere rather than face the truth that is always here. Why don't we see it? We have blind spots. And since we always have blind spots, we always need others to help us see what we don't see. For instance, one fellow claimed, "You wouldn't believe how humble I've become!"

Therapy doesn't eliminate blind spots. It helps us accept our never-ending blindness, so we can welcome feedback from those who see what we cannot. Terrified of our fear, we avoid feedback through illusions and defenses and become blind to the world outside them.

Yet blindness is not only a matter of what we don't see but also what we want others not to see. Rather than endure the darkness alone, we ask others to join us, to blind themselves by denying what is happening the way we do. Then we can delight in the bliss of mutual blindness: our agreement not to see what we don't want to see. This never works, for facts do not stop existing when we deny their existence. Through denial, we create our suffering, not seeing how we do it.

For instance, a woman proudly informed me that she had "asserted" herself by calling her husband an asshole.

"You shouldn't call your husband an asshole."

"Why not? I'm just being honest."

"What you call honesty, others would call cruelty. Remember that phrase: 'Sticks and stones may break my bones but words will never hurt me'? I don't believe that. Words hurt, and I suspect you hurt him when you called him an asshole."

"He needs to hear the truth."

"I'm sure he did, for the fact is that you called him a name—asshole. You didn't care what he felt. And he will remember the truth: you don't care."

She believed she had insight into her husband but was blind to the impact of her words, their meaning, and her cruelty. By arguing, she tried to convince me to join her denial and blindness. When I pointed out that he would experience her as cruel and noncaring, she said, "I didn't mean it that way. He shouldn't take it personally," as if meaning could be severed from speech and consequences removed from words. Alas, her contempt did have a consequence: a divorce.

We enter therapy not knowing what causes our problems. We start by saying, "I don't get it. I'm doing what I'm supposed to do, but it's not working." We have theories to explain our suffering, but those theories, like, "he's an asshole," turn out to be forms of blindness, and because we cherish those theories, we ask others to agree: "Don't you think he was wrong?"

If our therapists and friends love us, they will not love the lie that blinds us but reveal the truth it hides. If we love them, we suffer the truth they offer and live it. If we love our lie, however, we retaliate by criticizing, trying to push our pain into them: "That's not true! That's what *you* do!"

Since all of us have blind spots, we need others to point them out. And when they help us see what we don't see, we can do what we could not do before: embrace reality and receive its gifts. Until then we will be blind. Why? We blind ourselves with the lies we tell ourselves.

I Am Another You and Also Not You

Our psychological blindness results from the ways we blind ourselves through defenses. Nothing human is alien to us.[5] Yet every defense claims that feelings, thoughts, or desires are alien. We judge people for avoiding their pain through lying, ignoring the fact that we do the same. Or we pretend not to have specific emotions, urges, or problems. The psychiatrist Harry Stack Sullivan reminds us that "we are much more human than otherwise."[6] Each of us suffers the slings and arrows of life, loss, and death and tries to avoid what is.

We deny the humanity in ourselves that we judge in others. For instance, we might say, "The president is arrogant," "Wealthy people are greedy," or "Poor people are lazy." Each of us can be arrogant, greedy, and lazy but we are more comfortable when we imagine that a human trait is not in ourselves but in others we judge. But it's not true.

Fellow stumblers, deniers, and liars, all of us make mistakes and cause pain to others. These facts are painful to face. Instead, we try to step out of the world of humanity through our powers of imagination and pretend to be superior beings, watching *those* people, judging *them*, and rejecting *their* humanity. Without realizing it, we are judging our own humanity.

Every defense tries to kill our inner life or outer life. Each time we say our grief is silly, our desires are ridiculous, or our anger is ugly, we commit a murder. We can die of a single cut to the wrists or a thousand cuts to the soul, a psychological suicide.

When we meet a person, we find a different heart, a different mind, and a different part of life, which blows down our house of fantasies. In response, we can let go and accommodate life. Or rather than accept a different mind, we may dismiss it, showing contempt, or even entertain the most dangerous fantasy: "If I kill him, I can kill what he thinks." Every week fanatics try to kill thoughts and feelings by killing people instead.

These killings may be real or symbolic: whether it's the sarcastic attack of a pundit on a talk show, the wife who screams at her husband, or the father who beats his son, each attack tries to annihilate another person, another opinion, or another part of life. Yet just as we are powerless to stop death, we are powerless to stop life.

The Roman theologian Tertullian lamented two thousand years ago that "the first reaction to the truth is hatred."[7] Hatred tries to make reality disappear, and its constant failure to do so accounts for its violence; hatred always rises as if it only needed to become larger than life to overcome it. Fanatics, killers, and bullies believe they can eradicate an attitude even though the capacity for thought is born again in each child.

Yet in each generation too many children grow up in homes where they must silence their minds. The patient who suffered from psychological tyranny as a child may bring into therapy her childhood of soul murder:[8] "Will this therapist ask me to surrender my desire? Will I demand that the therapist surrender her opinions to prove she loves me? Can my mind and the therapist's mind coexist?" Often this conflict occurs in therapy.

A forty-year-old man consulted me due to problems in his relationships, problems he enacted with me. After I pointed out how his distancing behaviors with me reflected his distant relationships with women, he snapped, "This is a bunch of crap!"

"Do you notice how you are becoming sarcastic with me?"

"So what! I don't believe a word you are saying."

"It's okay with me that you disagree with me. Is it okay with you if I disagree with you?"

He shrugged his shoulders and said, "Sure."

"Obviously we have two points of view. You have yours and I have mine, and that's as it should be. Two minds in the same room. I assume that's okay with you?"

"Yes."

"If it's okay with you that we disagree, why do the extra work of sarcasm since it's not necessary?"

Surprised, he said, "I don't know. I never thought about it."

A few seconds later, he spontaneously described his alcoholic father, a tyrannical, sarcastic, and abusive man who had beaten him. Having been verbally abused by his father, he verbally abused me. His abusive speech, the apparent barrier, was the window to his past suffering. Rather than tell me his history through words, he presented his past through actions.

Bullies browbeat, abusive fathers batter, and fanatics kill, but they never eradicate reality. This man grew up to abuse himself and his loved ones while fearing they would abuse him. As an adult he became an abuser and the abused, perpetuating the pain he suffered as a child.

No matter how much he dismissed himself and me, his inner life always existed, even if it was hidden within his symptom of dismissal. Ever faithful, his anxiety kept pointing to the inner life waiting for his attention. In this sense, no one comes to therapy—our anxiety and symptoms bring us, hoping for the embrace that heals.

We want to get rid of the inner life that lugs us into therapy. Yet our task is to accept and bear how we are. As human beings, I am you, and you are me; we embrace each other as people who stumble, deny, and project. What if we are saved by embracing what we reject in ourselves and attribute to others? When this man saw that I was not his abuser, he realized that he had abused himself and others. As a result, he began to grieve over his losses and faced the rage he felt toward his father. Embracing his inner life, he stopped the abuse and dared to love once again.

People reveal to us other minds, thoughts, and beliefs—ours are not the only ones. Our image of the world doesn't contain their world, and our image of ourselves doesn't contain what they see. Our certainty disappears when we realize that our ideas about others describe our beliefs, not their being. The living person cannot be contained in a frozen idea. The man who claimed that what I offered was garbage saw his opinion, not me. He forgot that our reactions and ideas point to what is larger.

When we recognize that the idea of other people as separate and pathological is merely an image, our imaginary separation from the human ends. Until then, we suffer the alienation and loneliness that plagues our lives when we regard others as "not me."

Can I Pay You to Lie to Me?

To embrace other people, we must face their lies and our own. What if we are asked to lie? A man claimed he didn't need therapy. Since his friends thought he had a drug problem, he asked me to take his money so he could tell them he was in treatment.

It was a test: Would I offer a lie therapy or a real therapy?

He explained, "I just want to get my friends off my back."

"They aren't on your back. The truth is. And they keep pointing it out."

"If I don't hear it from them though, I can forget it."

"You can forget the truth. It doesn't need you to remember it for it to exist. No matter how far you run, there you are."

"Look. I'll show up and pay you. Then I can tell them I'm in therapy."

"But you won't be. You'll be in a pretend therapy."

"They won't know."

"But we will. You ask me to offer a lie therapy we know would not be real. You hope that by buying dishonesty from me, you can buy reality, but it is not for sale."

He smirked, "I won't tell anyone. You would be helping me out."

"I'd be helping your lie, not you. If I sell my integrity to you, I'll be a useless liar, another fraud in your life."

"I've seen therapists and done rehab before, and they've been happy to take my money."

"If I take your money for what you ask, I would be corrupt, not worthy of your trust. You would have no reason to trust me."

"Are you saying I should see someone one else?"

"You can find people who will help you lie if you try hard enough, but why hire a liar for a therapist?"

In therapy and life we meet with liars. We must be honest with ourselves that they are lying, and if we help them lie, we are lying to ourselves.

We hope to be healed, yet we fear what could heal us: saying, feeling, and facing the truth. Every one of us lies, and we will not drop our defenses just because a therapist points one out. We let go of them when the therapist is honest and neither colludes with our lies nor disregards our defenses. In a healing relationship we both must be honest.

We don't ask a liar to be honest. That is our lie, our resistance to facing his lies. The liar asks us to lie to find out if we are trustworthy. And when he lies, we must notice the urgency in his voice or in our hearts, for disappearing beneath the lies, the cries of his former potential become increasingly muffled and finally mute.

Devaluation

Another lie we tell is devaluation. One woman claimed I was useless, my comments were ridiculous, and the therapy was worthless. She devalued me, her close friends, and her family, alienating them and punishing herself with a lifetime of loneliness.

All of us will be devalued. It's nothing personal about us; it's something impersonal about the defenses devaluers use. It's not the hydrant's fault when the dog lifts his leg, nor is it our fault when people devalue us. People claim we have no value to avoid depending on the value we offer. Through devaluation they ward off the danger of depending upon others. Or people may deny our value to achieve an imaginary victory when they envy our genuine success. Unable to tolerate their envy, they devalue in us what they cannot find within themselves.[9]

When this woman claimed the therapy was useless, I asked, "Do you notice how you are devaluing me?"

"Are you saying I have to value you?"

"No. You can devalue me. It's a free country. But as long as you devalue me, you will relate to a worthless therapist and end up with a worthless therapy."

"This therapy is worthless."

"I'm glad we are in agreement. As long as you devalue me, this therapy will be worthless."

"I'm not getting anything out of this therapy."

"Of course. If you devalue me, you won't depend upon me, and you won't get anything out of the therapy. You can keep devaluing me if that works for you, but the therapy will end in failure."

"Why shouldn't I devalue you?"

"I'm your therapist, not your toilet."

"What if your therapy is worthless?"

"Is the therapy worthless or is your devaluation? You can devalue me. I can't stop you, but then this will become another failed therapy in the graveyard of failed therapies, and we will have to hold the funeral for the life you could have had. Why sabotage your therapy? Why perpetuate your suffering?"

Whenever we invite anyone to form a close relationship with us, our invitation will stir up memories of past relationships. In this woman's past, the ones she loved had hurt her. My offer of help stirred up mixed feelings: she wanted my actual care and feared my imagined cruelty.

Rather than risk being devalued as she was in the past, she devalued people in the present. She enacted her past: "Since you will abandon and devalue me if I depend on you, I will devalue you first."

When people devalue us, we may feel angry, as they felt when others devalued them. If we do not recognize this anger, we may turn it on ourselves: "Maybe she's right: I am not good enough." Or, intimidated by her, we might submit to devaluation as the patient submitted to her mother: "Since she gets angry when I talk, maybe she will like me if I stay quiet."

Sigmund Freud called the process of understanding and interpreting these dynamics "working through."[10] But recognizing the intense emotions that get stirred up in this process, the interpersonal analysts suggested we call it "living through."[11] In relationships, we face intense feelings and learn through living. That means we must face devaluation whenever it occurs, whether with a boss, a colleague, or a spouse.

When people devalue us, we might confuse our response of silence with kindness, but accepting devaluation is masochistic submission. The medieval theologian Thomas Aquinas once said we should never submit to another person because, in doing so, we invite her to sin.[12] Continuing to devalue hurts her, and when we accept devaluation, our resulting anger, depression, and despair hurt us. Submitting and retaliating do not help. What should we do? Tell the truth.

Devaluations are not insights but mind droppings. We are not useless; her devaluation is. Ironically, devaluation *reveals* our worth—what the devaluer envies and cannot tolerate receiving from us. Devaluation starves a person of any healthy human connection. It tries to kill off anything good that triggers envy.

To stop the murder of any relationship, not only therapy, we respond to hatred with strength.[13] A person can devalue us if she wants, but we have a choice too: we can part ways rather than collaborate with the cancer of her life. When we no longer defer to her devaluation, she gains a friend, or in this case, a therapist she cannot destroy but can depend on.

When people devalue us, we set limits to keep our relationship from becoming a latrine.[14] If we agree with a person's devaluation, we encourage her to commit a crime: killing a relationship. We should never submit to devaluation, even though life and therapy involve submission. We submit to the truth, not to a lie, and devaluation is a lie told to us.

We Die Once from Death but a Thousand Times from Self-Doubt

Sometimes people devalue us. More often we devalue ourselves. One woman said to me, "I always find fault with myself. I doubt myself all day long." Her self-doubt was self-hatred masquerading as "higher thought."

"I want to go to this workshop, but I am not smart enough."

"Could this be a self-critical thought?"

"What if I don't have what it takes?"

"Could this be self-doubt?"

"What if I fail?"

"Can we live tomorrow today?"

"No."

"Notice how you misuse this fantasy of the future to torture yourself today? It's as if you are saying, 'Why suffer then when I could suffer now?'"

She chuckled. "I do that a lot."

"Does this down payment of self-doubt punish you for wanting to leave your boss for a better job?"

She laughed guiltily.

When we doubt ourselves, we refuse to sit with our feelings to discover who will emerge. We preworry, filling the future with fears rather than going into the unknown of who we are.

We go through life with a candle, imagining that the light shows the world when it reveals only a sliver of life. Our true value lies not within the light but in the darkness. Who knows our future? No one. The task is to surrender to and embrace the unknown of ourselves.

Letting go of doubt's certainty, we realize how it blinded us to our true potential. And as we let go of the lie of self-denigration, feelings open our eyes so we can live the truth formerly hidden under self-doubt.

Gaslighting

Others blind us by asking us to agree with their lies, and we blind ourselves through false beliefs. Rather than admit that we can never plumb the depths of another person, we claim to know them, and that certainty becomes a new blind spot. To know any person, we start by recognizing that we don't. Not knowing is the precondition for learning about any person. It allows us to open ourselves to the mystery of another person. What happens, though, if we refuse to open ourselves up to other people?

A man consulted me regarding his previous therapist: "She told me my blinking eyes meant I felt murderous rage. Is that true?"

"No. That is mind reading, not therapy," I replied. Not knowing the depths of another person, we live with risk. We must drop our fantasies to relate to him.

This man continued. "When she told me something negative about myself, and I disagreed, she said this proved I was resisting. If I agreed to an accusation I did not feel was true, I gained her approval. It felt like a Catch-22."

"It was," I replied.

By interpreting disagreement as resistance, we can try to bully people into submission and call it "collaboration." Any fact can be misused to convince people that our projection is real. It's called "gaslighting" after the famous film[15] in which a man conceals and distorts the facts enough to convince his wife that she is going crazy.

Those who try to dominate and control another person do not help him find his words, they give him theirs—"listening" as ventriloquism. Instead of exploring his conflicts, they tell him what to do. When they are uncomfortable, they accuse him of "making" them feel what they don't want to feel. A therapist said to her supervisor, "This patient puts her confusion into me." The supervisor replied, "No, my dear. I'm afraid *you* are confused."

We blame others for our feelings without first examining our own. If we don't examine our feelings, we attribute them to another person. Then we equate that person with our belief: "Your blinking eyes mean you feel murderous rage." Now we relate not to a person but to an idea in our head.

Rather than push others to fit our ideas, we must become receptive, allowing what is happening to push our ideas to fit what is real. A student asked about her patient, "What will she do next?" I said, "I don't know. When therapists project what the patient will do, we avoid facing what we don't know. Our job is to be open to what we don't expect. If we're not open, we predict, and prediction is a fancy word for therapist projection."

We try to predict the future rather than live into it and discover the mystery of other people. By predicting, we control our anxiety about walking into the unknown. A man met a woman at a bar and asked for her number. Later he called her for a date, but she was distant and didn't agree to go on a date. When I asked what he felt, he said, "I feel overwhelming desire for her. I know she will love me." Of course, this was not "knowledge" but his belief. He didn't love her. He loved how he wanted her to be. He acted as if his desire was so great he could make what is real turn unreal. He kept calling her until she blocked his number. He tried to control her to avoid feeling his anger and grief: "I've been rejected." Controlling her meant he was at war with how she was. When he dropped his idea of how she "should" be, he stopped trying to control her and life. He became open to her, loss, and his feelings, embracing life as it was. Before, he thought he could reject the law of loss and rewrite reality. Then he let the loss and rage go through him. Instead of desiring what was not happening, he began to accept what *was* happening.

Instead of opening ourselves to life, we may fight it. Rather than open herself up to the patient in front of her, one therapist told patients they were "helpless, pitiful, crippled" or "filled with deep pathology." They became toxic waste dumps for projections masquerading as interpretations.

When I, with my history of destructiveness, can speak to you as a fellow stumbler, I no longer shine the light on *your* pathology but on *our* shared humanity. When we place our problems in others, we try to control our crises there. Meanwhile, we forget that we judge in others what we reject in ourselves.

This man who loved the woman who rejected him believed she should love his wish instead of her wish. He judged her for rejecting him when he rejected her desire. He thought she had not given him a chance. In fact, he had not given her a chance. He needed to accept her rather than love his wish. He had such a good fantasy script for her. He believed she had rejected him when he had rejected her as she was.

When we no longer ask other people to live up to our ideals, we can be real with them and ourselves and stop fighting life. In gaslighting, we try to change reality or make others not see it so we can live in our wishing well. In life, we embrace how others *are*, not how we *want* them to be. Until then, we resist life, thinking that life resists us.

Can *My* Love Melt *His* Defenses?

If it did, no one would use defenses anymore. Psychiatrists from Bruno Bettelheim[16] to Aaron Beck[17] have said, "Love is not enough." Why does this myth persist? It was our childhood strategy: "If I love mom and dad, they will love me."

Love is powerful; but the door must be open for love to enter the house. When defenses close the door, no one can enter. The child thinks his parents' hearts closed because of what he did. Blaming himself, he believes he must become a better boy, even more loving, for their hearts to open.

We still cherish that wish, hoping that if we are kind, others will be kind; if we are nice, they will be nice; if we love them, they will love us. Can love make facts go away?

Even in therapy we find this marriage of fantasies. A therapy website asks prospective patients, "What would your life be like if you had a father who knew how to love you and to guide you through different stages of your life? Would your heart be more open to love? Being re-fathered as an adult can be a nourishing experience for under-fathered men and women." What a lovely fairy tale: a therapist offers me the love my father didn't offer, and my past losses are magically eliminated.

Who has not hoped that love in the present could erase pain in the past? We wish love could do magic, and faced with enormous pain, therapists can wish the same. A psychotherapist years ago invited patients to put on diapers, sit in his lap, and suck on a baby bottle. He tried to reparent them to undo parental failures.

Alas, what is lost is lost. Refathering, remothering, and reparenting are not therapy but magic, attempts to fill the void in the past with fantasies in the present. We can't make the dead alive.

We can't rewind and rerecord the DVD of life. Unable to wipe out the past, we can only create a better present, accepting loss as part of life.

While we wish we could erase the pain of the past through love, we must face the limitations of life, loss, and death so real healing can occur. Therapy cannot replace what we lost, but it can help us let go of our barriers to love. Then we can mourn what was impossible in the past to form what is possible today.

It is impossible to melt defenses with love. Love is not water, and defenses are not ice. Trying to melt defenses with love is like trying to light a fire while our partner throws water on it. In this blind love, we don't see the whole person, only the part we want. Rather than embrace the fact—for example, "he rejects me"—we love the qualities we want and ignore the person we find. This is not a heroic act but hatred of the person. We try to become larger than reality through omnipotence: "I will *make* you love me while you reject me."

Trying to *make* anyone love us is not love but violence. We try to kill the person we meet and love the one we want. In fact, we don't love him. We love the *fantasy* we want him to become.

We wish our love were enough to heal, but if defenses close the door then love cannot enter. If our hearts are not open, we must open them. But if the doors of others are closed, we must go to other doors, open doors, where love can finally walk in.

◆

CHAPTER 4

Die Before You Die

In therapy and life, we face two deaths: the death of our bodies and the death of our illusions. To live into the truth, we must "die before we die." That is, we must experience the death of our denial and the stripping away of our facades, the images we have asked others to admire and reinforce.

Then the therapist and patient hold the funeral for the false self—the image we held of ourselves and asked others to hold as well. As we grieve the death of our self-image, our denial dissolves and our illusions evaporate. Then we begin to know who we really are, who we have always been underneath the lies.

Love and Death

For love to walk into our hearts, we must stop hiding behind facades. We are meant to live in the truth, yet we remain imprisoned by our self-image. How can anyone ever love us if they meet our facades instead?

The so-called "me" or identity is an image we present, an image we feed, and an image we ask others to feed as well. Junkies, hooked to our IV of self-esteem, we hope others will offer us pity or praise. Otherwise, they will see who we are. And when they do, the catastrophe occurs: our falsehoods, self-images, and identities dissolve.

Letting go of a cherished identity can be painful. An architect entered my office after her staff sued her for offensive and racist behavior. Outraged, she believed they were persecuting her. Her husband tried to calm her down, reminding her of times when her exchanges with staff had been too forceful, even caustic. She berated him.

"I notice you had a reaction to your husband's comment," I said.

She snapped, "Yes, he is against me too."

"What's the evidence for that?"

"He keeps taking their side."

"He wondered if your comments were too forceful. Were they, in your opinion?"

"Yes, but they deserved it."

"Okay. If your comments were too forceful, is he against you or this habit of forceful comments?"

"Oh."

"You're right: this habit is against you. Since your husband is not at the office, are your comments hurting you more than he is?"

"Are you saying I'm a hostile bitch?"

"No. I'm wondering if those comments are hostile to you, if they sabotage your wish to succeed."

"I guess you're right, but I feel like you are judging me."

"It's as if you are in the presence of a person who invites you to reveal yourself so he can misuse what you say to judge and condemn you."

"It feels that way."

"This image of a judge comes between us, and then you are with a judge instead of me." When she relaxed in the chair I continued, "People who are afraid I will judge them often suffer from too much self-criticism. Do you suffer from too much self-criticism?"

"Yes, I have been hating myself ever since I learned about the lawsuit."

"Would you like me to help you overcome that pattern of self-criticism so you can handle these problems from a position of calm instead of a position of fear?"

She longed for admiration, but her underlying insecurity led her to criticize others just as she criticized herself. As these attacks escalated, her reviews dropped, and her self-attacks increased, renewing the cycle until the lawsuit was the final blow to her self-esteem. She needed to bear the death of her self-image, the "perfect" woman, face her behavior, and accept the consequences. Instead, she raged that her husband and her firm did not support her.

They supported her but not her lie: the facade of the perfect woman. When we lose our self-image, we try to restore it and ask others to do the same. We lie to ourselves and ask others to lie, but life swirls around us, oblivious to our denial, beliefs, and outrage.

Her husband tried to stop her professional suicide: this was his act of love. Yet for his love to walk into her heart, she had to let go of her self-image of perfection. To see herself, she had to stop denying the facts. Rather than accept ourselves, however, we cling to our self-image, no longer open to this moment, the gift life has sent.

The architect later asked me, "Do I have to accept what you and they are saying?"

"No. You can reject what we say and see if that works. You do not need to move toward or away from reality because we are surrounded by it. All you need is to see the facts without rejecting them, manipulating them, or trying to fit them into your favorite opinions."

Communion with the truth changes us. Answers that worked in the past with other people are not the answers for today. We must let go of old answers to experience what we are avoiding.

As the architect listened to her husband, her staff, and herself, she accepted that she was not the image she pretended to be. Crying one day after recognizing her verbal cruelty, she shed her righteous indignation and felt her guilt instead, uniting with her humanity. "I thought I was better than that," she said.

When we embrace our pain, we experience therapy as a kind of subtraction where we let go of the known (our self-image) and walk into the unknown (what lives outside our illusions). As this woman let go of her facade of the perfect woman, she embraced herself as an imperfect human being but one who could love and forgive. And as she led with her love, a new version of her emerged.

As we let go of those identities, the imaginary veils between us disappear. We are right to fear love. It asks us to take off our facades. When we let go of our facades and grieve, we sink under our self-image into the wordless tears.

"I Am Afraid of Death"

A therapist said, "My patient with cancer is afraid of dying. How do I deal with that?"

"Could you be open to his fear and let him be afraid so he can learn what his fear is pointing to?"

"I've been worrying about how much time we'll have."

"Right. We don't know."

"I feel anxious. I wonder when to end the therapy."

"Death will do that. Is there a wish to end the therapy before he dies, so you don't have to sit with him to the end?"

"That feels right. I'm afraid he will ask me what death means."

"Could you sit with that question without having an answer for it?"

"He keeps wondering if death is a punishment from God."

"No. It only seems like a punishment when we live in an imaginary world where everything lasts forever."

Not willing to face life, we spend our lives in denial, running from limits and endings, even though no one outruns death. And only when it nears do we allow our denial to die before we do. Until then we use fantasies to ward off death.

Our wish for a world without loss causes continual suffering. We wait for the world we want, but the real world arrives instead. The deaths pile up: endings, illnesses, and losses of loved ones until we are next in line. These deaths batter our fantasies until our refusal to face limits breathes its last breath and dies.

This protest is not only individual but also cultural. Western culture has a death phobia. We flee the grim reaper through fantastical slogans: "Just do it!" "You can be anybody you want to be!" "You can have it all!" These fantasies are drummed into our heads as real, but the limits of life and death turn out to be real instead.

The terror of the end rarely appears as fear because we ward off our fear of death through eating fads, plastic surgery, hair coloring, the life of *Homo consumens*, and the frantic urge to do more and "be" more. Meanwhile, our skin sags, our hair grays, and we do less and less, unable to be what we are not: younger and further away from death.

A dietician friend of mine said, "Eat right, exercise, and die anyway." If we view dying as a battle to win, we will lose. No matter what diet we eat or plastic surgery we endure, we soon become worm food. No longer refusing life, we face living into death. The following fable describes this path.

A salt doll walked along the sea for the first time. The doll asked, "Who are you?"

The water replied, "I am the ocean. Come in and find out."

She walked into the waves and, just before dissolving, gasped, "Ah, now I understand who I am."[1]

Our grief is not a thing we need to contain, manage, or understand but to live into so our illusions can dissolve. This allows the real to emerge. As we grieve the loss of our illusions, we become one with what is. Dying dissolves our denial, shifting our priorities from illusions to the truth.

We do not die by choice, but we can choose to face our feelings about it. We join our friends, our colleagues, and our loved ones by holding their hands while they enter the darkness and learning that we are dying too.

Falling into the mystery of death requires us to sacrifice our cherished illusions. When grief dissolves our denial, it dies before we do. As the dying goes through us, we live while dying. Death is always present because every moment dies and is replaced by another.

Dying invites us to let go of denial and to be open to what is: we are always living into death. And when sharing this experience with a dying friend, we give him what he *can* take to the grave— love. To love and to be loved by a person crossing the threshold is truly a blessing. It challenges our capacities to embrace the moment and leads to even deeper grief at the end—revealing our humanity. As we sit, holding his hand, loving him, knowing he feels loved, we feel what Joseph von Eichendorff points toward in his poem "Im Abendrot":

The great peace here is wide
and still and rich with glowing sunsets:
If this is death,
Having had our fill of getting lost, we find beauty, No regrets.[2]

"I Want to Die!"

While most of us die due to illness and decline, some choose death to escape their pain. When love dies, we may say, as a depressed man did, "I want to die. I can't go on." How does a therapist overcome a patient's urge to die?

She doesn't. She accepts and explores his yearning to die. Open to this expression of the human heart, she does not treat the patient like an object to be fixed but as a person to be loved. She extends her hand, not a pill. For if she tries to convince him not to kill himself, she distances herself from his pain and from our universal urge to surrender when our hopes run out. Telling him to live when he wants to die is not listening.

I asked a depressed patient, "When did you start wanting to die?"

"My girlfriend and I were engaged and had set the wedding date," he replied. "We went to a party one night and had too much to drink. I was out on the patio with my friends when I noticed she wasn't there. I started looking for her, opened the door to a bedroom, and saw her having sex with the guy who owned the house. I couldn't believe it. I walked out, got in my car, and drove home. She called me the next day and apologized, but she said she was in love with this guy and wanted to call off the wedding. I figured maybe she'll get over it."

"What's the feeling toward her for betraying you?"

"I feel depressed."

"But the feeling toward her?"

"I love her, but I hate myself. I wish she would come back."

His wish to kill himself was double-sided. On the one hand, wanting to kill himself turned rage toward his ex-fiancé back upon himself. He dies, not her. On the other hand, wanting to die also meant he wanted to live: "I don't want to live this way. I don't want this facade of pure love anymore. Living a lie is unbearable."

He wanted to die rather than suffer the death of his dreams. His dreams of his ex-fiancé's return were a graveyard where he waited for a dead relationship to come to life. He could have let his hopes die but he considered killing himself instead.

In therapy, we held a funeral for the dead engagement, so it could be blessed and buried. Then he could relate to the ex-fiancé he had rather than the wish he had about her. Life is not worth living if we are living a dead dream. Only by burying the wish could this man find a way to live into what was.

We do not embrace the truth by holding ourselves outside of it and observing it but by becoming lost in it as salt dissolves in the sea. As his illusions dissolved in his grief, he let go of his attachment to an idea, the girl he wished his ex-fiancé were. Instead, he embraced the woman she was, which freed him to find the woman he eventually embraced and married, the woman who, in turn, embraced him.

This man was right: a dying life is not worth living. If he had killed himself, he would have avoided the pain of facing the dead engagement, but he also would have lost the chance to let go of an idea in his head and find a woman in the world. The therapist helped him let go of the fiancé who had already let go of him. This is why we say someone is attached to an idea: this man held onto the idea of a woman who wanted him because the real woman didn't. He was not attached to her but to what was not there and not real.

We can even be attached to the idea of suicide itself. A woman met me for a consultation after having been suicidal in spite of therapy that lasted for twenty years. When I said she deadened her feelings, she replied, "Maybe I want to be dead."

"The good news is, if you want to, you can. The ingredients are available in every drug store. Neither I nor your therapist can stop you from killing yourself. Even in hospitals people kill themselves. If you want to commit suicide, you can. This choice is always available, but why does such a talented person want to be a dead woman living in the casket? Why?"

The pain blossomed across her face and she burst into tears. After this consultation, for the first time, her suicidal depression lifted.

Her wish to die revealed her longing to live. What if the wish to die is the first step in the journey? Could the intent to end a dead life point to the wish to live a real one?

Underneath her longing to die was the wish to come out of the grave she had dug for herself. Her pain told her, "Your way of life has been a death in disguise." In a sense, she could not commit suicide because she already lived as a dead woman. She was right to despair: living a lie is hopeless.

When listening to a person who wants to die, find out why. Something does need to die. Not the person, but her way of dying while alive.

How Death Talks to Us

While some seek a death they can avoid, others try to avoid death when it is inevitable. How does a therapist talk to a dying person? The following transcript of a role-play shows how I helped a student who was stuck in her work with a woman dying of cancer. She asked, "How do I talk to her?" We agreed to do a role-play in which I was the therapist and she, the woman

She started, "I'm here because there's not much time."

"Yes, can you accept that?"

"There is so much to do."

"And not enough time."

"I don't know how much time I have."

"Of course."

"I see how I keep disappearing. I look in the mirror, and I see half of myself."

"You're dying; I see that too."

"It's terrible. I wonder how many times I will come here."

"We don't know. This could be the last."

"No, no, no! I have planned my last trip to Paris, and I'll be here next week."

"Mhmm."

"I could die suddenly. The worst thing is when I think that I will live like a vegetable taking medications."

"That's possible."

"It's not acceptable for me."

"Reality is not acceptable. Can you accept that you can't accept life as it is?"

"I can't accept that for many years I haven't lived the way I wanted."

"You can't accept your past, but the past is what it is; it doesn't need your acceptance."

She paused. "It came to my mind that I'm probably afraid."

"Can you accept your fear?"

"It's difficult."

"Can you accept this difficulty of accepting your feeling?"

"I can't do anything else."

"Reality is here whether you want it or not. What do you feel as we face death and your fear?"

"Emptiness."

"Of course. You want to be empty rather than full of death and cancer and fear. We have a few sessions in which I can help you. Do you want me to help you before you die? It's okay if you want to hide behind your emptiness."

"I'm getting a stomachache."

"It makes you anxious to face death, to face the goodbye."

"It's the first time I saw it. It is so difficult for me to allow this."

"Can you accept that it's difficult to allow death, to allow reality?"

"I knew the prognosis. Only now do I feel how close it is."

"You're full of death. You're full of feelings. And we have today and hopefully a few more times to face these feelings together before you die. You have this chance, if you want to let down the wall before you die. Even if you regret your past, you can die in peace without regretting the present. Without the wall we'll have a chance, but it is painful. If you want to fight reality, if you want to fight death, if you want to hide behind the emptiness, I will respect your wishes; and when you die I will bless you and your memory."

"I'm not empty at all. I have so much, and I'm afraid I won't have time."

"You have this moment. Why wait? You've waited your whole life, and waiting has created your regrets. Why create more regret? Would you like to leave this prison of loneliness while you still can, before you die?"

She cried, "This is terrible, thinking this is the last time. What's the point? Why?"

"Can we accept your wish not to connect? Shall we accept your wish to distance yourself from me, and to be alone? Can we accept your wish to die alone? It must be important to hide from me and remain the unknown woman."

"No. I'd like just once to feel full acceptance and closeness, and I'm so afraid this is the end. It's not worth it."

"Do you want to be intimate with death? Death is intimate with you. Death is crawling through your bowels. Death is crawling through your liver."

"I can't stand it anymore."

"Can you accept death?"

"I have no choice."

"That's true because death has accepted you. What do you feel when we make room for death to be here?"

"I'm a little bit less afraid."

"What do you feel when we make space for death, allow death to be inside you, and allow death to be inside me?"

"It starts being mine."

"Your death. What feelings do you notice when you accept your death?"

"It's strange, but it's peace."

"Nowhere to go, nothing to do, no one else to be, only you and me here with death."

"As if it has always been with me."

"Death was always with you and for the first time you know it. What do you feel when you accept that death has always been with you?"

"Peace and relief. I thought that maybe I'm ready to say goodbye. I'd like to say goodbye to so many people. Also these unfinished scripts, I want to finish them."

"We are always unfinished. You mentioned saying goodbye to your friends; by saying goodbye to your friends, you admit you love them and that they count."

"More than at any time before."

"Your love had meaning, they mattered to you, and your love matters now."

As the pain spread across her face, she said, "It hurts."

"This pain is the womb from which you are being born."

"It's a lot."

"Yes."

"I'd like to tell you that it's all right now," she said. Our role-play ended.

Therapists do not give us insights but invite us to experience the truth so insights can arise from within. Therapists don't tell us what we don't know. They tell us what we sense but don't want to bear alone. They present reality in a manner we can listen to, accept, and live through together.

◆

CHAPTER 5

Being the Opening
for Truth

As we let go of our lies, we become more open to the truth. But more than that, we experience ourselves as a welcoming openness. When we embody openness, our seeing, hearing, feeling, and listening change, and with these changes, the barriers dissolve between us and what is.

Attention as Openness

When attention to others disappears, and we focus on our ruminations instead, we drift far from dialogue and even further from Simone Weil's proposal that attention is a form of prayer.[1]

Why pay attention, and what is attention's role in therapy? We pay attention to other people's preconceptions to break us out of our own. The poet Goethe suggested, "Man knows himself only to the extent that he knows the world; he becomes aware of himself only within the world and aware of the world only within himself. Every new object, clearly seen, opens up a new organ of perception within us."[2]

Every time we let go of a lie, we get closer to what is. The therapist interrupts defenses—habits of thought, customary commen-
taries, popular projections, the barricades we erect to separate ourselves from our loved ones—so we can listen. We become open to
them—not our ideas about them. We should never consider ourselves as finished, complete, or understood but as "evolving, grow-
ing, and in many ways as something yet to be determined."[3] The
question is not who we are in contrast to those whom we reject but
who we are as this openness to those we formerly rejected.

Change Me!

Rather than be open to life so *we* can change, we ask life to change
and be open to us. A woman yelled at her children, "Stop doing
that!" A college student, infuriated when his professor flunked him
due to his late assignments, threatened, "I'll sue you!" When life
does not change in response to our orders, we may order others to
change us. This can happen in therapy.

A CEO barked at her therapist, "I don't want to feel this way.
Do your magic!" treating him like a slave who should serve her
every need. At times, we wish therapists could sprinkle pixie dust
upon us, and therapists can wish they were wizards with wands
too. Who hasn't wanted to transform others magically to remove
their misery?

A magician tries to change you without relating to you. Magic
arises while he remains unfazed. Between you and him, we find a
void where a relationship should be. No exchange occurs in which
his presence changes you and yours changes him.

Magic is such a contrast to love! Love is dangerous, opening us up to others, stripping off our illusions, and mobilizing our potential. Can we let reality and our feelings move through us?

To escape that danger, we ask others to change or ask others to change us in order to stop the change already happening inside us. We engage in a perpetual home renovation project with ourselves when we say things like "I hate the way I am," or with others when we say things like "Please change for me!" What would happen if we took ourselves and our loved ones off the torturous carousel of so-called self-improvement?

The CEO's instruction "Do your magic!" revealed her problem: a wish to be manipulated as she tried to manipulate others and life. "Treat me like an object. Don't relate to me as a person. Teach me to control people so I can escape the fateful communion with them." People are not possessions to rule at our will; they are not property to exploit as we wish but springs to drink from, gifts to cherish, and mysteries to plumb.

We Are Not Ideal but Real

We usually go into therapy because we want relief from our pain, or because we want to know ourselves better. Rather than bear our experience, however, we may hope that therapy, medication, or meditation will change our experience. At worst, we may even hope that therapy will cure us by turning us into someone else.

We invite violence to ourselves. A businessman endured much suffering under his demanding, critical father, for whom he had never been good enough, smart enough, or successful enough. His father always found a flaw. At the end of our therapy, he said, "I'm not disappointed with the therapy."

"Of course you are," I said.

He smiled and laughed. "Yeah, it's true."

"How has therapy been disappointing?"

"I don't know. I had hoped we would have deep emotional experiences like you see on television or the movies, and I would recover childhood memories that would explain everything."

"I've seen those movies too, but we didn't experience that, did we? Deep feelings came up, but no new memories."

"Maybe I asked too much from therapy."

Rather than point out how he wanted a supertherapist like his father wanted a superson, I said, "Although you hoped for an extraordinary result, this has been an ordinary therapy."

He chuckled.

"What feelings are you having about being with such an ordinary therapist?"

He laughed. "I guess I expect a lot from people, so I get disappointed."

"And I guarantee disappointment here."

He laughed. "Maybe I could borrow that, so I could tolerate others being disappointed with me."

"You're a natural at disappointing people too! I didn't know you had such a talent," I jested.

"I guess that's inevitable isn't it."

"Since desire is infinite, one thing we can guarantee is disappointment."

"I've been trying to avoid that."

"You tried to be everything for everybody, wore yourself out, resented them, and wanted to go on strike."

He spent his life trying to transcend conflict by trying to become who he thought people wanted him to be. And while they may have loved the imaginary image he presented, they couldn't love him because they never met him.

He hoped his father could love a real son in the world, whereas his father loved an ideal image of his son that existed only in his mind. The businessman believed he must become ideal rather than real so he tried to eradicate the differences between himself and his father's ideal image. The businessman thought he was flawed because he didn't live up to his father's image of perfection. In fact, his father's belief in perfection was itself the flaw.

"What if your flaws are just what is? You are not meant to be ideal but real."

We are always flawed when compared to the ideal. We cannot flee from what we are. This man grew up with the belief that he should leave, become someone other than he was, and return as the ideal son to be loved. He began therapy trying to be the ideal patient to please me. Instead, I had to help him be himself, not my or anybody else's ideal.

We were not put on earth to be satellites circling around other people, even if they want us to be. We can rotate around a person's ego, pretending to be him but we will never become him. This man's father was in love with an image of the ideal son, the perfect son, and the son who has never existed. Our virtual image of how life should be is a story we tell based on our imagination. Meanwhile, life keeps coming instead.

This man needed to embrace his experience to be a real person instead of pseudoideal. After therapy, he realized he was merely human and would always appear disappointing if compared to ideal fantasies. There is no cure for our humanity.

This man tried to love his father's ideal and hate himself, but none of us can be ideal. In love we open up to our imperfect humanity. And what is imperfection but humanity as viewed through the spectacles of perfectionism. Taking off those spectacles, we become open to ourselves, others, and everything that is "not perfect."

Being Present in Therapy

To be open, we are told to "stay in the moment." Yet where else can we be? Even if we are lost in our daydreams, we are lost *now*! We look into our stories, rather than look right here.

Wilfred Bion said that therapy is an act of faith that we can be transformed by becoming at one with the emotional truth of this moment.[4] How we are is what we have been looking for. No need to *be* present. Each feeling, fear, and act of avoidance is how we are present. We don't need to be different but to sit with who we are.

One man had to sit with death. He descended into the cellar with his five-year-old son and discovered his wife hanging from a rope tied to the rafters. A few days later he told his therapist that he wanted to die. The therapist asked for my help. He played the role of the patient, and I played the role of the therapist.

"What would you like my help with today?"

He answered, "I can't find myself."

"It sounds like you did find yourself; you found yourself full of grief, loss, and the image of your wife's dead body hanging in the cellar. Because you found yourself, you want to lose yourself. Who wants to find death?"

"I can't believe she did this."

"You can't believe she killed herself."

"She is always present in my thoughts. We've been married for fifteen years. And we were so happy. Now I have moments of anger toward her."

"Of course. You are angry with her for abandoning you and your son. And how difficult it is to be angry toward a woman you love."

"I don't know how long I'm going to live. I don't see the sense of my life."

"There is great sense in your life, but it's very painful, and you wish you could die to end your pain."

Every word he spoke showed us where to go. Everything we needed was present in each moment. His anxiety pointed to the feelings we needed to embrace for his healing to begin.

Who wants to accept death? Who wants to feel rage toward a wife who killed herself? Who wants to keep living when our beloved has died? Yet life always whispers, "Will you welcome your experience?"

When his wife committed suicide, this man's idealized images of her, his purified images of himself, and his images of their future together died too. Naturally, he thought of physical death to avoid the psychological death, the death through which he would be reborn but at a cost. In the cellar, not only the memory of her body hung from the rafters, so did his dead dreams.

Freedom From or Freedom To?

Welcoming our feelings, thoughts, and dreams is a big task, but it's easier if the therapist welcomes them too. Accepting our inner life means accepting everything, not only the easy parts—love, joy, and happiness—but even our resistance and refusal to collaborate.

Slouching in his chair, a man described his goals for therapy. When I asked if he wanted to work on them, he stared at the ceiling and groaned.

"Well, in a sense, I don't want to. I guess I don't know if I am willing to commit or able to spend a lot of time dealing with all the other issues I have."

Accepting his reluctance, I noted, "You are not sure how committed you want to be."

"Yeah."

"I appreciate your being so straightforward. You can be as committed or uncommitted as you want."

"I guess I want to make sure. There are things in my past that would be fruit for years of therapy potentially. I guess I am not committed to spending that much time in therapy. But I want to make sure that I come out of this with a tangible improvement."

He mistakenly thought the issue was whether he should commit to therapy. "Since we are combining forces together, we need to find out how committed you are to yourself."

He looked up at the ceiling, smiled, and said, "How committed to me; yeah, I guess that is interesting."

"Are you worth it?"

Chuckling and looking up at the ceiling again, he paused and said, "Um, sure I'm worth it."

"What do you feel as you say that?"

He smiled and then said, "It seems like a form of marketing."

"What are you feeling when you say that you are worth it? What gets triggered inside when you say that?"

"Part of me says that I should immediately say yes, I am worth it."

"What do you feel when you say that you are worth it?"

"Ambivalence about whether I want to spend a huge amount of time and money on it."

Since he still mistakenly wondered whether to commit to therapy, I explained, "The question is, do you want to commit to yourself? You are ambivalent about how committed to be to yourself. You have one foot in and one foot out."

"Yeah. There is some truth to that."

"You are ambivalent about how committed to be to yourself and what you want."

Looking away, he responded, "I don't know whether this is the same, but there is a lot of self-editing that goes on."

We often edit our inner thoughts and outer speech to fit what we think others want to hear or how we want to appear. Sadly, though, through self-editing we stop being open and listening to what rises up within us.

"Are you worth being listened to?"

"I guess. It's funny. I don't feel it that way. I guess it is a want of confidence in terms of expressing my views and doing what I want to do."

"Unsure whether you want to commit to yourself, whether you want to edit yourself or to listen to yourself, and whether to go for what you want."

"Yeah."

Since he still had not committed to himself, I asked, "How much would you like to hold yourself back?"

He sighed. "I'm not a totally free agent. I cannot jettison everything I want. I guess the question is, how do you get to the point where you can be honest with other people without feeling like you are going to destroy the things that matter to you." His eyes filled with tears.

"Your feelings about being honest and fearing the impact that would have on others are important for us to notice. We need to be as honest as possible, and if you fear that I would be harmed, we need to pay attention to that."

"No, it's not that. It's honesty and," he paused, "it's a wish that I could be more self-confident. Why does it matter what other people think or feel?"

"Do you wish you had more faith in yourself?"

He sighed and looked away. "Sure."

"Does self-doubt get in your way?"

"Yeah."

"I assume you came of your own free will, and you weren't dragged here by anybody, right?"

"Right."

"You came of your own free will. Yet as soon as you say you want to commit to yourself and get to the bottom of your difficulties as quickly as you can to achieve your goal, you doubt what you want."

"Yeah."

"You are at war with yourself. You wonder whether you should listen to yourself or to these doubts."

"I'm not sure what the problem is. It is hard for me to know if that impulse that I'm experiencing is the real one."

In response to his confusion, I helped him differentiate himself from his self-doubt. "You've doubted yourself for so long that you don't know which is the real you, the impulse to doubt or the one that is being doubted."

"That is a scary thought."

"What are you feeling?"

He smiled and rolled his head. "I don't know."

"Take your time. This stirs up a lot of emotion."

"It's funny. I've talked with people who are self-aware and empathic enough that I'm aware I have these issues. It's not like a horrible revelation, but what is my real identity? What do I really want?"

"If you don't want to do this, I have no right to ask you to do it."

"No, I don't doubt the utility of therapy."

"You are at war with yourself, wanting to commit to yourself and doubting whether to commit to yourself, as we decide whether we should join forces and commit to you."

He smiled. "You are right. I'm thinking, 'God, this could be a long therapy.'"

"If you doubt the utility of committing to you and hold out on committing to you, you can make this therapy as long as possible. You can drag it out for twenty, thirty, or forty years if you work it out right." He laughed as I continued, "If there is anything you do to make your therapy unnecessarily long, we have an obligation to make sure that doesn't happen."

When a therapist sits with us without demanding that we change, love enters the room. The therapist can describe our defenses and the cost they inflict, but she can't take them away. We can keep our walls of defenses as long as we want. That's why people can have years and years of therapy without having changed a bit.

The therapist unconditionally accepts our walls because she must face the facts to be effective. Her radical acceptance of our resistance questions our self-rejection. When we reject the therapist, she remains curious, accepting our rejection without demanding that we accept her. And for the first time, we may experience a desire for movement from within.

This man did not want to commit to therapy or to his own growth. He thought he was avoiding the trap of long-term therapy. In fact, he was entering the trap of self-doubt, seeking freedom from his feelings by doubting them. This is an impossible goal since we can never become free from what we are.

For the rest of our lives, we will experience anxiety, sadness, anger, shame, love, and joy, clouds crossing the internal sky. Our freedom will not come from doubting our inner life but from accepting it as it passes by.

Through bearing the emotional flowing we are, our awareness takes us away from our feelings to what perceives them. We discover we are also the emptiness in which feelings appear, the quiet in which chatter happens, and the sky across which the clouds pass.

Through defenses we seek freedom from our emotions and lead a life on the run.[5] We long for freedom in forms it never takes: freedom from conflict, feelings, life, and death. And we seek freedom in places it is never found: our fantasies. This man was imprisoned by self-doubt; he was a lonely observer doomed to sit beside the river of life but never swimming in it.

In contrast, we do have the freedom to love and embrace what is. When we stop running *from* reality and embrace it, we find the freedom we are looking for.

The Danger of Listening

We may regard listening as easy, but in fact, it is hard: by opening ourselves up to another point of view, we run the risk of changing the way we see ourselves, another person, or even the world. To ward off the risk of being changed by listening, we engage in pseudolistening where we argue with people to change *them*. What if listening changes *us*? The philosopher Heidegger proposed that we suffer because we have forgotten how to listen to others or ourselves.[6] We have forgotten our essence, he said, because we have forgotten how to listen.

One woman had trouble listening to herself. She started talking with racing speech, scattered thoughts, and twitching feet. "You are talking rapidly," I said. "Do you notice that too?"

"I didn't notice that, but I want to talk about something else."

"Talking rapidly is a sign of anxiety. Are you aware of feeling anxious in your body right now?"

"Yes, but I want to tell you something else."

"I'm sure, but do you notice how you ignore your anxiety and invite me to ignore your anxiety too?" Her eyes were swimming in tears, so I asked, "What are you feeling under the words now?" She sobbed.

She listened to the chitchat in her head, not to the anxiety in her body, and neglected herself and her feelings. Although not her conscious desire, she invited me to ignore who she was underneath the distracting chatter.

We may not listen to ourselves or to others. Another woman described a conflict with her husband. He complained that she always talked over him. "Why should I listen to him again? I know what he will say."

She didn't know what he would say; she knew what she *thought* he would say. I don't even know what I will say. What we say emerges as we say it. That's why we listen. Even when loved ones appear to repeat themselves to us, they may not be repeating what they said but *what we failed to hear*—a testament to their faith in our wish to listen.

This woman listened to her belief and talked over her husband. Meanwhile, her husband could rightly say, "You are not listening to me." She thought she heard what her ears perceived when she perceived what her mind projected onto him. She kept saying to him, "See?" imagining that his mind was closed. In fact, she closed her own mind by relating to her ideas, not to him. What if our beliefs are not insights but the barriers to insight?

A therapist presented a case for supervision of a man who she believed was severely disturbed, a disturbance for which I could find no evidence. The therapist, convinced of her view, continued on her campaign. Perched like a bird of prey, scanning for the right facts to pounce upon as "evidence," she argued with him, trying to dominate him and make him submit to her projection: "See! *That* is who you are." For her, his words were ideas to be shot down. Listening became a form of target practice.

To listen, we must accept a person as someone who deserves to be heard, whom we no longer dismiss, debate, or dominate. Then we can surrender to the fact that other people have other points of view. We think we see the whole picture when we see only our own perspective.

A Zen abbot created a garden to illustrate this point. When viewing the Zen rock garden, Ryōanji, from the veranda, we can see only fourteen of its fifteen stones from any given view. To see the fifteenth stone, we must move, but having moved, we lose sight of another stone. We learn through moving that the whole picture cannot be seen from any one viewpoint.

When we open up to another person's perspective, the possibility of dialogue brings us to the next error in listening: listening to "know" a person. The problem is that we never will. In fact, we never know ourselves completely.

When a person says, "I know exactly what you think," she looks at her projection, not you. She equates you with her idea about you, but you will always be unknowable.

As we accept the limits of our knowledge and our perspective, our listening becomes a kind of surrender. We surrender our beliefs that we have known or will ever know anyone completely. Our beliefs regarding other people are revealed as images in the mind, carefully cultivated creations, and delicious but delusional substitutes for the real. Once we realize these images are just images, we become open to another person.

When driving in the summer, we experience the illusion of water shimmering on the road ahead, but it recedes the farther we drive. This experience of driving toward an ever-changing landscape is like love: illusions drop away repeatedly so we can experience the "ever-receding horizon" of the depths of our beloved.[7]

Whereas the eye creates visual illusions, the mind creates emotional illusions. In psychological life, we do not see people but our preconceptions about them. And preconception is a polite euphemism for defense.

Defenses are the ways we distort, filter, block, and interpret the world, generating patterns of ignorance we call "truth." While they are almost always an adaptive response in childhood, when used in other relationships, they create our suffering. For instance, if I make excuses for failing a test, I will mistake my excuses for the facts, failing to see the rest of the truth: I didn't study enough. If I am rude to my wife and she objects, I might project that my wife is "sensitive." I will see my belief but not my rudeness.

While we ignore what is here, we are surrounded by it, stumbling over the realities we didn't see. "Why did I fail that test?" or "Why did my wife get irritated again? She is so touchy!" When defenses turn our gaze from the real, we see only the unreal: our mind-created images. If we are to see what is real, our false perceptions must dissolve.

Rather than face what is happening, we ask others to agree with us to avoid facing facts that contradict our beliefs. We think, "If enough of us share the same idea, my belief will win." We fight for the last word, but it's pointless; when the last breath crosses our dying lips, we discover that the last word always belongs to reality.

We argue instead of listen when others disagree. "Don't confuse me with the facts; I have an assumption going here!" We think we are listening when we are expecting, judging, and evaluating. We compare what we hear to what we believe. When we give up expecting, judging, and comparing, we begin to listen.

Negative Capability

We go through life not knowing the answers. Who will we become? What do other people think and feel? Faced with the fear of the unknown, we fill in the void with false assumptions. This "knowledge" is projection.

The poet Keats referred to negative capability,[8] which is the ability to sit with what we do not know until experience brings the not yet known to the surface. Not knowing is the well from which all knowledge is drawn. And nowhere is this more apparent than in marriage.

A man offered derogatory insights about his wife during our therapy session. I asked, "What do you say we make some stuff up about her?"

Startled, he laughed, realizing, "I do that a lot." He projected onto her so much that he saw not her but his projection.

We can only speculate about other people, for by definition, they are unknowable. Projecting onto loved ones does not illuminate their uncharted interior life. Yet like the early mapmakers who filled in their images of the New World with mythological mountains, nonexistent cities, and fabled features, we create elaborate fictions filled with imaginary motives, which purport to represent the hidden worlds of others.

It's hard to admit "I don't know" when trying to understand another person, and it's so easy to fill in the gap with our fantasy. And since the fantasy is ours, it feels like a fact. "If I feel it, it must be true," we think.

We live surrounded by the unknown. We *are* the unknown. So are the future and the stock market. For instance, unable to bear the unknowability of the stock market, we turn to irrational optimists or irrational pessimists, the "bulls" and "bears," who sell us stories of fear and greed, plying us with fictions. Their conflicting fantasies merely reflect our refusal to tolerate not knowing. Likewise, when we can't tolerate not understanding another person, we make assumptions.

A middle-aged woman who felt victimized by others said, "I need to tell you, I didn't like what you said. You must have been angry with me. You seem empathic but under the surface, you're not. I should have known you would be just like the others."

My crime? I had a different opinion. She wondered why I disagreed with her. Unable to understand why I disagreed, she assumed I wanted to hurt her. She used this story, with slight variations, to explain every relationship she had. She always attributed goodness to herself and evil to others. We might call this her pattern of ignorance, an ignorance created by ignoring the unknown of the other person and filling it in with hostile motives. Once she ignored the fact that she did not know my motivations, she took the second step: filling the void with her assumptions. She could never see me as long as she stared at her beliefs, the barriers preventing her from learning.

Rather than learn through living and feeling, she tried to avoid experience by pseudothinking.[9] Her problems were due to what she "knew." To learn, she needed to *unknow* her assumptions: the lies into which she tried to stuff life, her loved ones, and me. She could face that she didn't know my mind, or she could cram me into her fantasies. Then she felt trapped with a disfigured, distorted image, a cartoon from which she could expect only the predictably horrible.

We may project to avoid our feelings or we may project onto the therapist so he can playfully agree to be the location where our problem is analyzed. Then the therapist must also have this negative capability, the capacity to sit with the unknowable. A schizophrenic man came in one day and said, "Jon, I've figured out your diagnosis."

"Oh really?" I said, "What's that?"

"Satyriasis: uncontrollable sexual appetite for women," he said, giggling.

"Oh, my God, how did you figure that out? Even my analyst didn't catch that."

Chuckling, he said, "Oh, it's obvious."

"Wow! That's embarrassing. I thought I had that pretty well hidden. Do you think there's any hope for my condition?"

"Yes, but it will take a lot of therapy."

Inviting him to be the therapist of "my" problem, I asked, "What do you think is the cause?"

"You probably didn't get enough breast-feeding as a baby."

"Do you think that's why I'm obsessed with breasts?"

"Yes." He laughed and continued to analyze my "problem" for twenty minutes until he said, "Well, enough about you. I want to talk about something else."

"Alright, if you insist. What's that?"

"I have trouble talking to women."

Initially, he didn't need me to interpret that satyriasis was *his* problem; he needed me to be the place where his problem could be played with until he could later examine it within himself. I had to have faith that he would find a way to reflect on his inner life after having projected it onto me. Likewise, we must have faith that we will come to understand people when we don't understand them yet, when we face the unknown. Paraphrasing Simone Weil, what if the original sin is our tendency to fill the void, the mystery of another person?[10]

Without faith and openness, unable to comprehend another person, we assume, attribute, and project. A woman complained, "I don't know why my husband doesn't want a new house. He is insecure and too worried about debt. He is irrational when it comes to money." She tolerates the mystery for a second and then fills in the unknown with her assumptions. The danger is that she will be open to her notions, not to him.

This woman thought the unknown, her husband's not wanting what she wanted, was a question requiring a solution. She tried to kill the question with false answers. What if questions are not problems?

Living with Questions

We do not need to answer questions. We need to allow, experience, and live the questions of life: "What will happen?" "Who is this person?" "What do I want?" Premature responses avoid the experiences of life through which we learn the answers. If we cannot tolerate learning through living and feeling, we start lying through thinking, creating the false knowledge of our assumptions.

A middle-aged man described a Father's Day card he received from his daughter in which she wrote, "I am soooooooo lucky to be your daughter."

"That is such bullshit," he sneered. "She only wants to go to France with me on vacation, since I invited her. She wants to use me. She doesn't care about me."

"Notice how you take her expression of love, turn it into shit, and make yourself lonely?"

"Love?" he barked. "She doesn't love me; she's always angry."

"Since you reject her love, it's no wonder she gets angry."

"I asked her, 'Why did you write that? What did you really mean?' And she gets pissed off."

"You accuse her of not loving you. Then you ask her to disprove your accusation, to defend herself. When she gets angry, to you that proves your assumption, when in fact it proves that accusing her makes her angry."

"Don't I have a right to know?"

"When you project, whose job is it to deal with your projection? Is it her job or your job?"

His head dropped onto his chest. "I've ruined her life."

"What are you feeling?"

"I feel bad."

"What is that bad feeling?"

"Guilt. Nothing can be done."

"Nothing can be done about the past. All you can do is admit what you did, apologize, and repair the damage." His head sank into his hands, tears streaming down his cheeks, shoulders shaking.

His accusations blinded him to his daughter's love and imprisoned him in a fantasy world that he had not seen until the tears opened his eyes. He filled in the void with his assumptions and asked his daughter to defend herself from motivations she did not have and actions she had not taken. If she argued with him, she lost because he held onto his ideas, and projections never include what they are designed to exclude.

His daughter, like every person, was someone whose heart he would never fully know. Rather than sit with what he didn't know, he made stuff up, paid attention to that, and no longer saw her as she was. He listened to the answers from his mind to avoid listening to her, revealing that he loved his thoughts more than he loved his daughter. When we choose our assumptions, we reveal our fear of the truth.

We hate not knowing. Hating the questions of life, we dig up past answers to past questions. Instead, this father needed to let go of old answers to begin to open himself to the new question, who is my daughter? When he let go of his assumptions, accepted her, and listened to her, he began to learn who she was.

Not knowing her was not a problem but the path. As we take this path of accepting the unknown, we feel uncomfortable. Yet this discomfort is a message from life inviting us to love another person.

He thought he should have answers, but he needed to let go of his false answers. Then he needed to accept and love what he didn't understand in his daughter. When we maintain that same openness about people, stop making stuff up, and tolerate our experience, we can come to know them.

This father, like all of us, had to accept what he feared: the unknown within another person. To love her, he had to learn that his daughter was a mystery, not a pile of projections. The author Jose Saramago reminds us that "inside us there is something that has no name, that something is what we are."[11] Embracing his daughter—the invisible, the unnamable, the unknowable—the father learned to love her instead of his assumptions.

When we let go of the false answers in our mind, we live the questions of life. This father had to free his daughter from his prison of projections. Likewise, we must live with our questions, whether they are about life, a person, or ourselves, as we would hold a bird lightly in our hand: "when we squeeze it, it dies."[12]

Deep Knowledge: Past Lives

A middle-aged psychotic woman excitedly reported new insights each week. One week she learned she had been Cleopatra in a past life. Another week she discovered she had been Anne Frank. Week after week, she described her past lives; the illusory fame was no doubt balm to her soul after the excruciating losses of her career, friends, and marriage during her long descent into psychosis.

One day she came in with a smile on her face, sat down, and announced, "I was Mary Magdalene in a past life."

"Oh, I've always known that," I replied.

"How did you know that?"

"I loved it when you washed my feet."

Shocked, her eyes opened wide, and she burst into laughter.

Since she felt too much pain and had too little capacity to bear it, she had to ward off an unbearable reality and retreat to a bearable fantasy. Through play, I joined her delusional world so that for a moment, she felt less alone with a person who understood the function of her delusion: to bear unbearable loss. In our unspoken way, we knew the wisdom of Sigmund Freud's insight that delusions try to restore that which was lost and will never return.

Later when she lay dying of cancer in the hospice, she said, "See, I told you the Nazis were after me. They knew I would give birth to the Messiah. So they gave me cancer." Smiling through my tears, I surrendered my therapeutic ambition and accepted her delusion, the thread that gave meaning to her now, the larger than life grandiosity being the only talisman she could cling to as she faced death, other than that other tendril: our relationship.

At the funeral, her children expressed their gratitude for my work with her: "This must be hard for you. I know how much she meant to you." At the time I thought they had projected their grief onto me. In fact, I had projected my grief onto them. It *was* hard for me. She had her delusion and I had my projection. All of us struggle with the losses of life. Sometimes, the deaths of life are too great to bear, and the mind breaks under the strain. For others of us, when our illusions break, our identities die, and what we are underneath arises.

Letting Go

Unable to bear the losses of life, we may console ourselves with delusions. But if we bear our losses, we always experience a letting go, not an intentional one we can force but one that comes to pass.

A woman lamented, "My mother has been diagnosed with cancer, and the doctors don't know when she will die. It could be a couple of days or months. Should I make sure she gets lots of food? The doctor says it won't make much difference. What can I do to keep her alive? The nurses say I need to let go. Do I need to let go of her?"

When those we love are dying, we want to keep them alive, but death visits anyway. We don't know what to do because nothing stops death.

Books tell us to let go, yet we need not let go of those we love. We need to embrace what is happening. When we embrace dying, letting go happens naturally. Trees embrace the winter; leaves fall to the ground.

Death does not need us to let go for our loved ones to let go of us. What do we let go of? When we hold our loved ones' hands in the casket, an inner movement stirs. Their lives, our longings for what could have been—everything slips through their hands and ours. We don't let go, but their cold fingers tell us they have let go and invite us to let go of what is no longer in our hands. They listened to death; can we listen to their hands?

What was not cannot now be. While our loved ones breathed, we held the hope for our future. Once they died, our hope did too. We need not let go of them; they will rest in our hearts forever. The tears we shed and the cries we howl remind us of our capacity to love, which continues after our loved ones die.

Surrendering to reality, we merely face the facts. Our denial already lost the battle against what is. There is nothing we need to do and no ideal way to be. We are rivers of grief with unpredictable turns, gushing until our mourning rests in the ocean of acceptance. We cannot push the water because this flowing of love is who we are. As we flow down into our being and come to a rest in the quiet and stillness, we realize that a dying loved one's final gift to us is this invitation to acceptance.

CHAPTER 6

◆

Embracing

To heal, we must embrace the truths we avoid and the feelings they evoke. These truths we embrace include our inner life (our feelings and anxiety and the ways we avoid them) and our outer life (reality). In this embrace, we discover who we are and who we always have been underneath the lies we tell ourselves.

Whom Did I Marry?

Falling in love is such a wonderful adventure, but within a few years something strange occurs. Our spouses appear different, disappointing. Why?

In my case, I fell in love with a fantasy and over time met my wife instead. What a crisis! I was disappointed she was not the same as my wish. I believed she should be the way I thought she should be. No one asked me, "Jon, who made you God?" As a result, my suffering (and hers) was protracted.

Then I realized if I couldn't love her as she was, I should let her go so someone else could. It was not her job to be my ideal. I should live up to my ideal if I think it's that important. I thought, "That's not possible either."

I went to the internal divorce court and divorced my wish. This painful proceeding extended over years, but once I had divorced my ideas, I was able to marry my wife instead. To a degree, I was more in love with my wish than my wife. I saw the value in my longing, but this blinded me to the inner beauty underneath her "flaws," flaws meaning departures from my desires.

Magazine titles tell us "How to Be the Perfect Partner," "34 Moves to Sexually Awaken Your Spouse," and "How to Revive a Marriage." But no article says relationships die if you try to manipulate each other into being ideal mates or Olympic sexual partners. No column says marriages perish when you love your ideas instead of your spouse.

When we love our story of who our spouses should be, we try to give them the script. "Why are you always late?" "You shouldn't watch so much television." "Why don't you wear this instead?" "You've had enough!" These instructions, freely and compassionately offered, accompanied by deep insight into why they fail to follow them, often take the form of fights. Our spouses realize we want our image, not them, and for some mysterious reason, they become angry.

When we say things like "You would be happier if you woke up earlier," what we really mean is "I would be happier if you weren't you and turned into who I want you to be instead!" The mate keeps showing up instead of our demand. Then we whine, moan, and complain, looking for books and articles to tell us how to argue in marriage. What if we are fighting *reality*? Will this fight make my fantasy spouse appear and my real spouse disappear?

A conflict can enact our divorce from life. We never have a fight with a person but with what he or she represents. A woman nagged her husband for eating junk food on vacation. For him, vacation was a time to enjoy a few potato chips and Oreos. For her, he shouldn't want junk food and shouldn't eat it.

She assigned herself the role of the food police and lectured him on the health consequences of his snacking. Or she gave him dirty looks, priding herself on her "self-restraint." Her fighting attempted to make him go away: "Don't think, act, or be this way." She was no longer interested in her real husband. She was interested in him becoming her fantasy: "Stop being the husband I have and become the imaginary man I want." If he did not become the mate in her mind, she would have to let go of the imaginary twin who wanted what she wanted. Unable to love the man she had, she remained married to the image in her mind and made their lives miserable. Finally, he realized that her marriage to this image was a divorce filing with him, so he finalized the divorce by leaving her.

Why does our spouse show up and not our wish? Do we have to divorce our wish? Must we get engaged to reality and marry this imperfect person? Marriage means that we divorce our fantasies to embrace the person we married, the person who will never be our fantasy.

Is Love a Projection?

What is love? We can reduce love to merely a sexual instinct, self-interest, or a positive emotion. Yet if we consider only sexual attraction real, love itself becomes unreal. If love is unreal, the qualities we see in our beloved are merely our projections. Is that true?

Do we pick our loved ones by comparing them with other products on Match.com? If we treat dating like a mate market, where we regard people as commodities, we shop around for the best deal—the package with the right attributes—and pick a person off the virtual shelf. But selecting a product is not the same as loving a person. Love draws us in by what we cannot name or describe, but only sense and feel—the otherness of the other.

In contrast, self-love lacks the essential transcendent dimension of love: the ability to glimpse a person's inner value and respond to her interior beauty. For instance, a narcissistic woman mistakes her self-love for love of her husband. She becomes angry when people insult him but not because they hurt him. She thinks they hurt her, since she views him as an extension of herself.

A loving woman is not preoccupied with her reaction; she feels compassion for her husband's pain. It's not about her. She sees her husband so clearly she does not need to project onto him. She does not need to convince herself to love him because she cannot help doing so.

Is her love for him a feeling? Feelings appear and disappear in response to what triggers them. They're states of mind. Love, on the other hand, is more enduring. Although we feel fluctuations of love within us, those fluctuations are not fleeting clouds that appear and disappear in the sky but the shifting tides of an ever-present sea, expressions of the love we are.

Love is not mere pleasure like we find in a warm bath. No one has ever married a bathtub. We could reduce love to a need, a wish, or sexual desire. These forms of illusory love are based on a craving in us, not a response to the beauty in our beloved. If he merely serves our need, he is an object we use, not a person we love.

Satisfying a need, such as drinking a glass of water to end our thirst, decreases our interest in the water, ending our movement toward it. However, love intensifies our sense of awe, drawing us closer to our beloved. Satisfying an appetite is finite, but exploring the mystery of our beloved is infinite.

When asked why you love your spouse you become tongue-tied. Words like "kind" and "sweet" may be true, but they are so inadequate; the preciousness of your spouse cannot be contained in partial details.

Love is unsayable and even *undoable* because when you love someone, you are no longer a separate person "doing" love to your beloved. Instead you feel a current of love, a current that arises the moment you stop regarding your beloved as an object, a thing, or a category in your mind. She is as she is, separate from all of your ideas. You love her, not some image of how you want her to be. She loves you, not an image you ask her to love. She and you are a mystery loving a mystery. Those blind to love never meet the mystery they are with because they chase the image they desire.

A man of means came to therapy to show his wife that he wanted to resolve the issues that led to his extramarital affair. Meanwhile, he lied to his wife, saying he would be faithful to her, and to his mistress, promising he would leave his wife. The problem he brought to therapy was that he wanted to keep his mistress happy, so she would not tell his wife about the affair. For him, women were objects to be bought, used, and discarded—every person was a commodity, each with its price.

Such a man could not perceive anything but means and ends; his two-dimensional world was devoid of sacrifice, encounter, and mystery. Trapped in his fantasies, he no longer lived in the world. He set himself apart from reality. His wife and mistress were objects to use and have, not persons to love and cherish.

He could not allow either his wife or his mistress to be as they were. Instead, he demanded that they be who he wanted them to be. He thought that his wife should have accepted his promise of fidelity as a substitute for it and that his mistress should have accepted his promise of marriage as a substitute for a wedding. In both cases he said, in effect, "Pay attention to my words; ignore my deeds."

He could not meet these women as people because, for him, they were things to use. He did not realize that when we treat people as things, we relate to fantasies. Only when the ones we love are no longer fantasies in our minds, do those people become real to us—then love begins.

Love takes delight in the inner beauty of the beloved. This inner beauty calls out to us, and we respond to these depths our words can never grasp and toward which they can only point. The beloved's inner beauty calls forth our love, which in turn brings out more of that beauty. As the theologian Dietrich von Hildebrand says, "The value flashing up in another person pierces my heart and engenders love for him."[1]

When we treat our loved ones as treasures, others might claim that we are blinded by love and that what we value is an illusion. Love does not generate an illusion of value. Devaluation strips away the value of a person and treats the resulting illusion of no value as real. Interestingly, devaluation is an alienated form of love, the love of images. The devaluer wants to devalue someone and *relate to that devalued image*. He is secretly attached to this defaced form. By loving the image, he becomes unable to see the inner beauty of others, suffering from a form of spiritual blindness.

In contrast, when we love our beloved, we do not love an image in our mind. Nor do we present an image to love. Nor are we obsessed with getting our beloved to admire us for being loving. For in love, we and our beloved are love itself. We are responding to and from our depths, not to or from our facades.

In love, we are not the focus. "With whom is the lilac in love when it scents the air; the pear tree when it produces abundance;

the lark when it whistles curiously its song?" as Robert Wolfe asks.[2] I am not a *giver* of love to someone outside of myself who is the *receiver*. Saying "I want you to love me" means, "You are an object to fulfill my desires." Viewing people as objects separate from us who must be conquered is not love but delusion.

In love, we no longer find an image of me and an image of you but a presence, since the images are lost in the love like sugar cubes dissolved in water. In love there is no lover or beloved. What we are transcends ideas of you and me. We are not separate from love; the imaginary separation is an artifact of thought. Is love a projection? No. Devaluation is.

Why Do We Shout in Anger?

A Hindu saint visiting the Ganges to take a bath found a group of family members on the bank, shouting. He turned to his disciples, smiled, and asked, "Why do people shout in anger at each other?" His disciples thought for a while until one of them said, "Because we lose our calm, we shout."

"Why should you shout when the other person is next to you?" asked the saint. "You could just as easily speak in a soft voice." His disciples offered answers, but none were satisfactory. So he explained, "When two people are angry with each other, their hearts become distant. To cover that distance, they must shout to be able to hear each other. The angrier they are, the stronger they have to shout to hear one another over the increasing distance. What happens when two people fall in love? They whisper because their hearts are so close. The distance between them is either very small or nonexistent."

The saint continued, "When they love each other even more, they need not even speak. To gaze into another's eyes is enough when two hearts beat as one. When you argue, do not say words that push others away. Or else a day will come when the distance is so great you will not find the path of return."[3]

We never shout at a person but at the image we have placed upon him, for instance, the image of a person who doesn't want to listen to us. In fact, his ears are fine. If we assume that he does not want to hear us, we will yell at our projection. We shout at someone whom we *believe* does not want to listen to us. Yet we do not want to listen to him, for if we did, we wouldn't yell at him.

Relational Knowing

In a therapy session, a man described having sex with his girlfriend while fantasizing about another woman. When we explored his problem he wondered, "Who knows? Maybe they have met each other somewhere. It's always possible."

"You speculate about them, creating imaginary fantasies for us to relate to. You invite us to copulate with your ideas, but you are not present with me."

"Like I do with her," he said, referring to the way he made love to a fantasy woman in his mind while having sex with his girlfriend.

Copulating with his speculations distracted him from his girlfriend's love. Rather than let the act of lovemaking dissolve his walls, begetting greater closeness, he used imagination to separate himself from her embrace. He had sex with many women, but had made love to none. An eternal wanderer in life and a sightseer in love, he had never dared call any heart his home.

We can treat another person like an object we put outside ourselves and inspect. Or we can open ourselves to a mystery, a person from whom we no longer distance ourselves and whom we never fully understand. We cannot convert the essence of a person into a thing we think about.

A person is not a static piece of plastic but a living, changing being. When we love a person, we relate to the one we know, the one we will come to know, and the one we will never know. She is not a piece of clay we mold into our image, but a person with whom we enter into communion.

When we cut ourselves off from a person, we cling to what we believe, freeze it, and claim, "This is who you are!" We no longer find the person, but fondle our idea of him. Using our ideas to "grasp" a person is as futile as using a butterfly net to catch the wind. In contrast, love keeps shattering the concepts in which we tried to contain a person. Love reveals who this person is beyond our ideas and beliefs. As we become intimate with those we care about, we begin to respect their transcendence and mystery.

Later in the session, the man who fantasized about other women during sex was moved to tears during a moment of emotional intimacy with me, and he said, "It's strange. It's wordless inside, and I don't know where these tears are coming from."

"This wordless silence is you."

"I never felt this before."

"This is home. You can stop wandering."

"I start doubting whether this is real."

"The mind doubts reality, but you always exist under the chatter."

Underneath his false knowledge was his wordless being. We sat with his silent tears until he said, "I'm not saying anything."

"Your eyes are telling us what your lips cannot say."

The man's tears revealed what he was underneath the words, ideas, and labels. And in this openness he began to realize that he was none of those ideas but the awareness that perceived them. The therapy helped him notice a space within himself that he had not recognized before.

How sad it is when despair blinds us to the potential inherent in any human being. If we fail to relate to the unknown, we will never learn of the potentials in another person. We fail to hope.

A therapist in training lamented, "My teachers at school and our clinic say that people cannot benefit from treatment if they are too old, too feeble-minded, too sick, too disturbed, or if they use drugs and alcohol. If an elderly man asks for my help, I'm supposed to tell him that therapy can't help him." Handed the gun, she was asked to pull the trigger and become a killer of hope.

A therapist cannot know in advance whether therapy will enhance our lives. A good clinician will not decide based on his projections but on his explorations; he will talk to us to discover what we cannot see in ourselves.

Emily Dickinson reminds us of hope's delicate quality: "Hope is the thing with feathers."[4] This fragile tendril that keeps people alive should never be crushed. In psychotherapy we embrace not only what the patient can see in himself but also what he cannot yet see. In that way, we extend our faith and hope as a loan.

Alcoholic, schizophrenic, borderline, and mentally retarded are categories and diagnoses, but who are the people underneath these labels? A therapist never treats a diagnosis but the broken heart, which is its cause. Once, a medical intern rushed to one of my colleagues in panic and begged her to get a woman to return to the hospital. The patient, a hypochondriac, had asked the intern to examine her three times that week. The intern told the patient that he would check to make sure that she was not having a heart attack. She ran out of his office crying.

My colleague called the patient and invited her to come in for a consultation at the hospital. She talked to the patient and noticed an important fact in her chart: the patient's son had been murdered a year before. She said to the patient, "Your doctor didn't realize that you are not suffering from a heart attack but from a broken heart." The patient entered therapy and made rapid progress. With her son gone, she had no one to pin her love on, so she satisfied her "hypochondriacal" needs by volunteering at the hospital, where she delivered books, and read and talked to patients. The patients became her son, the hospital her home, until the therapist helped her mend her broken heart.

The last thing we need is a therapist to reinforce a pathological belief that we are hopeless. We need a pilot to help steer us toward realistic hope. For even if the therapist cannot offer the highest hopes, she can at least point us toward our highest potential.

When we have no hope for ourselves, we are blinded by defenses we don't see and lies we can't identify. Despair, no matter how well rationalized, represents the refusal to relate to the potential buried under the pathology. Discovering the essence hidden underneath is the art and gift of listening. If we give up on and forget another person's essence, hope dies.

The therapist helps us find a path to new possibilities. No matter how much we may limit ourselves, she sees how we can transcend those limits. The despair of this moment is but a partial glimpse of ourselves, for the rest of who we are lives outside our defenses. The therapist's faith in us means that she sees what we don't see: who we are beyond our blinders.

Psychotherapy helps us see who we are, the vastness that exists outside our self-image. Freed from our illusions, we get a glimpse of who we are and take up the task of listening to our depths.

Insights or Outsights?[5]

Relational knowing differs from cognitive thinking. That's why people often question the value of cognitive insight. If those insights were so helpful, self-help books would long ago have cured the world.

When we have intellectual insights about people, we talk about them as if they were objects. This is not true psychotherapy but a disturbance for which real therapy can be the cure. What if people invite us to form this kind of distant relationship?

I noted how a former gigolo was distancing himself from me and asked him what he felt toward me that made him want to put up this barrier. He replied, "I don't know."

"Saying 'I don't know' is how you hide, but then I will never get to meet you. What feelings are coming up toward me that make you hide from me?"

"I have no idea. I mean, I could throw something out for you."

"Yes, and then you become a psychological gigolo. 'Maybe Jon would like to hear this or relate to that.' Then we will have the same destructive gigolo relationship you had with your girlfriend. What feelings make you put up this barrier of the psychological gigolo?"

"There could be any of a number of feelings, I guess."

"Notice how you take the position of an observer? You sit outside this relationship and watch this interaction between me and a man who has your name. You are outside the therapy, observing it. This has kept you a tourist in life, always on the outside looking in."

His eyes teared up.

"What feelings make you hide behind the facade of the detached observer?"

"I think I do that a lot. I remain the observer, the judge."

This man distanced himself from everyone around him—even from himself—and led the life of a detached observer. Rather than feel his feelings, he had spent a lifetime detaching from them. He repeated the insights others had offered but to no effect. These insights were "outsights."

We begin therapy with diverse insights from parents, teachers, and friends, ideas that may drown out our inner voice. These insights are not understandings from within but outsights, views from the outside. When others pay attention to their opinions instead of our feelings, they listen away from our being and create outsights. If we listen to their outsights, we become deaf to ourselves.

How can we listen to ourselves so true insight is possible? We hear with our ears, but that is not adequate. We need to listen with our entire being. In this welcoming openness, we do not figure out the truth; we live it together by bearing what we feel without rushing to words, premature formulations, or new lies.

While listening to our feelings, can we bear their message? By bearing our feelings, we finally speak from our depths. Our task might be summarized as, "Listen to what is underneath the thoughts, and hear what those who 'know all' cannot."

What Is Relating in Therapy?

To understand therapy, we must ask whom therapists relate to: a list of symptoms, a diagnosis, or a personality disorder? No, therapists relate to the person hidden under the symptoms, the symptoms caused by the divorce from his inner life.

Then therapists encourage us to undo that divorce and embrace our feelings. Using defenses over the years, we forget our desires and passions. This is the price of self-neglect, a habit used by the following woman. She reported a conflict with her boyfriend but said, "I don't want to look at it."

"You have a problem, and you don't want to look at it. Is this how you neglect yourself?" I asked.

"I don't think it's that important."

"You don't think *you* are important. You dismiss your problem and yourself."

A flash of sadness crossed her face. "I get it."

"Do you notice how you invite me to neglect you too? When you ignore your problem, you ask me to ignore you and say, 'You aren't important. We can dismiss you.' Why?"

Her eyes tearing, she confessed. "I'm used to it. I do this with men all the time."

We engage in self-neglect and call it strength, but it's self-hatred. This woman invited me to ignore her and perpetuate the dismissive relationships she had with men. She tried to forget her being and asked me to do the same. When I refused to collude with her crime of self-neglect, her feelings arose, and she spoke with a new voice. Therapists focus not only on what we say but also on how we listen to our feelings before we speak. Can we bear our feelings so our speech becomes full of what is inside us? When this woman bore the pain of her self-neglect, an insight emerged: "I do this with men all the time."

When We Do to Ourselves What Was Done to Us

When we come for therapy, we bring the history of our suffering— sometimes in words and sometimes in the ways we treat ourselves. If others have hurt us in the past, we often hurt ourselves today in invisible ways, perpetuating our suffering in the present. The therapist, seeing our subtle forms of self-harm, doesn't go on a fishing expedition into the past. Instead, she points out how we hurt ourselves in the present.

In the following excerpt from our first meeting, a woman said that she was moved by what I had told her.

"What do you notice feeling as you let me help you?" I asked. "You just came out of hiding."

She sighed. "I was afraid I would start crying."

"Why not? Wouldn't it be better to cry than to be anxious?"

"Yes. It was very moving for me. At that moment, I thought, 'I hadn't met a man before who would hear me.'"

"Are you willing to let me hear your tears?"

"I'm not going to cry anymore."

When therapists see how we reject our feelings, they comment on the cruelty we inflict upon ourselves, a cruelty we don't see. They neither collaborate with our dismissal nor judge us for it. Instead, they compassionately point out how we cause our suffering.

"Do you want to stay anxious instead? Why be so cruel to your tears? Don't they deserve love too? How long do your tears have to be rejected? When do they get to come back in the house? They must be getting very cold outside. How much longer do your tears have to suffer out in the cold before you let them back in? You don't have to worry if I will reject you. We have to worry about you rejecting yourself and your tears."

"I had this thought that we should talk about something important instead of crying."

"You have this thought that you should talk over your tears and ignore them, but I know you didn't come here to ignore your pain."

Her face filled with sadness.

"Let the pain go through."

"I'm afraid the tears will never finish when I start crying."

"When you never let the crying start, the crying never stops. It's why you have to let the tears out so they can finally stop and so your pain can come to an end."

"Maybe I will let myself cry, but I cut it; I stop it."

"You cut off your tears. You cut off yourself. You reject yourself and your tears. Isn't it sad that you reject yourself like this? Why perpetuate your suffering? Why reject your pain? When does the sad girl get to come back into your arms? Let the tears go through."

She sobbed for several minutes.

"The thought I have in the moment is, 'Oh my God, I am sitting in a negative way and crying.'"

"And there's more pain. Don't punish yourself; don't criticize yourself. Let the pain come out. You don't have to hold it in anymore. You have the capacity to let your heart be healed. That's it. There's more where that came from. So much pain. So much suffering. Let it out. That's why you came."

"I'm ashamed."

"Oh, how sad! When you are most in pain you slap yourself with words. Oh, please don't hurt yourself like that. You've suffered too much already. Let's not add to your suffering. This is not a time to shame yourself; this is a time to have compassion for your pain. This is not a time for cruelty to you. You don't need any more suffering. How sad that you were tempted to punish yourself for revealing your pain and sadness. Don't hold back."

"It's always like this."

"You've always punished yourself for letting yourself become close to another person?"

"First, I heard that I am doing everything ugly, too much. I exaggerate. I make things up."

"They punished you for revealing your pain."

"For anything. Even for joy."

"You were punished just for being emotionally alive."

"Mhmm."

"Go ahead and cry. It's okay to be alive now. Let yourself be alive. And who judged you for being emotionally alive?"

"Mother and father, both of them."

"Is that where you learned to punish yourself for being alive?"

"That's how it happened."

She did not need to tell me her history of neglect; she enacted it through the ways she dismissed and ignored her feelings. First I had to help her see and let go of her habit of self-neglect to allow the grief and pain to rise up and heal her. Then we could face the feelings toward her abusive parents, especially the anger she turned on herself. She had always protected her image of them as all good and regarded herself as all bad. Through this tragic violence toward herself, she revealed the love she had always felt for them but at the cost of her own well-being.

Once she faced these feelings deeply, her depression lifted for the first time. And as she let go of her self-neglect, her self-compassion grew, a compassion that extended not only to herself, but to her parents, and, especially, to her son. In the depths of her feelings, the judgments, thoughts, and insults of the past dissolved. She realized that she was greater than the misunderstandings of her parents. Now she lets her parents have their problems without making their problems her prison.

Lies We Tell That Lead Us to Fail

"Therapy is bullshit." That's how one man began his consultation with me. He had been in psychotherapy for thirty years without benefit. After this marathon of failure, his therapist referred him to me for a consultation. The patient said he came because his therapist sent him, and added, "I'm skeptical that you can do anything." As we explored the reasons for the previous failure, he said that he had 99 percent given up on therapy. When I asked why he came, he said, "Hope springs eternal." I asked how he experienced this hope. He said, "I don't." Then he told me that therapy was bullshit and therapists were bullshit. In the meantime, he said, "I'm in prison, waiting to die."

His contradictory statements began to make sense as I realized that although he came for help, he took a passive stance and waited to be rescued by friends, girlfriends, and therapists. In his stance, he asked others to express hope and desire, and take responsibility for him. When they tried, he opposed them, argued with them, and defeated them. Rather than express his hope and his desire for him, I had to reflect back his lack of hope and desire. The following excerpt shows how we can tell the truth and embrace it.

He began the session by expressing contempt for me as another "bullshit therapist" who would do no good. On the one hand, he wanted help. Since he feared that if he trusted me, I would devalue him, he devalued me and himself instead. For instance, he described himself as hopeless, helpless, worthless, and ugly.

I asked, "Could this be a form of violence to yourself, this self-criticism?" His eyes teared up. "I never thought about it before."

Although he had spent a lifetime attacking himself, he had never thought of it as a way of being violent to himself. Seeing this for the first time took him by surprise. Recognizing his cruelty to himself allowed him a split second of self-compassion.

"This contempt for me is nothing personal. It's just your way of showing me how you show contempt for yourself." He sobbed again. After he felt this grief over the violence to himself, however, he attacked himself virulently, justifying each insult. Every comment I made he tossed aside as worthless.

Eventually, he said, "I feel like giving up."

"If your story works for you and you think that you are ugly and hopeless, and you believe that, it makes sense to give up."

"Therapy's not going to help me, but there's always that thread of hope," he said flatly.

"You don't sound hopeful, and you don't look hopeful."

"There's a hope for a hope."

"You seem convinced you are right. If so, the best thing to do is to give up hope and wait for the end."

"Yeah. Probably, but I mean it's one of the only games in town, so I go to psychotherapy. What do I have to lose but money?"

"You are asking yourself to do something you don't think will help. Why waste your money?"

"Maybe I have the wrong therapist."

"You could always go shopping around."

"Shopping doesn't work. There's no one out there."

"Why go looking?"

"There's a little bit of hope."

"You don't sound hopeful. You don't look hopeful."

"I'm not aware of it. I hope for hope."

"In a way, therapy is defeated before it even begins."

"It probably is. Yeah."

"That's okay. I can't succeed with everybody."

"Would it help to read your books?"

"This is about giving up. If you've already given up on yourself, why try?"

"I haven't entirely given up," he said passively. "And please don't ask me how I experience this. I don't know."

"Are you sure you haven't given up?"

"I'm 99 percent sure I've given up."

"I can accept that. You must have good reasons for having given up. I have no right to argue you out of something you have thought through. People with certain experiences realize they have to accept their lot. It may no longer be the time for hope. The time for hope may have been in the past."

"I don't know what you are driving at. Maybe you are saying there is no hope and why not give up and stop going to therapy. Maybe you're not saying that."

"Since you've given up 99 percent."

He interrupted, "Are you playing devil's advocate?"

"No. I'm only reflecting reality. If you've 99 percent given up and are waiting for therapists to take responsibility for you to get better, you're wasting your time."

He thought I was trying to trick him. He didn't realize how the lies he told himself had been tricking him for thirty years.

"I've been doing this for thirty years."

"You've done this for thirty years. Whatever you've done hasn't led to change. If you keep doing that, nothing will happen. You will need to do something different. If you've given up 99 percent and are waiting for a therapist to take responsibility, it doesn't work."

He sighed, "So you're saying if I've given up 99 percent, I'm ill advised to go into therapy."

"Right."

"Maybe I ought to stop altogether. All I need are some drugs to feel better. I guess I was hoping you could convince me otherwise."

He hoped I would argue with his lies. Then the conflict would be between him and me. Instead, I had to tell the truth. Then the conflict would be between his lies and reality.

"You've had thirty years of therapists trying to convince you. If you've 99 percent given up, you have good reasons. Therapy doesn't work under those conditions. If you are waiting for the therapist to make you have hope, that isn't going to work."

"Would you speculate as to how I could have hope?"

"Only you could know. There must have been a moment in your life when you had hope and when you gave up. Something must have been crushing enough that you turned against hope."

"It was gradual."

"That happens with people."

He sat up, so I continued, "I'm trying to give you honest feedback. You don't want to spend another ten years fruitlessly. Therapy doesn't help everyone."

"What does one do if therapy doesn't help?"

"That's one question you are facing. Perhaps use medication and see what medication offers."

"If I get my knee fixed and exercise regularly to produce endorphins, I can exercise my way out of it."

"Exercise is good."

"The other way is to fake it until I make it."

"People do that too."

"They say you should do what you enjoy doing, but I don't enjoy doing anything. So you're saying therapy won't do any good for me."

He mistakenly thought therapy would not do him any good. In fact, his strategies of giving up, taking a passive stance, and being defiant would not do him any good. He was right. The lies he told himself were not helping him.

"You've tried giving up for thirty years, and you're presenting me the evidence: thirty years and no results. How you are approaching therapy isn't working. If you want a different result, you need to do something differently. Only you can know what you could do differently to get a different result. Maybe there is nothing you can do. Only you can know."

"You throw the ball in my court. I'm pretty much helpless."

"If you're helpless, we have to accept that you can't do anything. Some people are physically or psychically crippled, and if that's true for you, you would have to accept a crippled life."

"You're being honest, aren't you?"

"Right. There are crippled people. If you have genuine disabilities, you will have a crippled life. Again, I don't know. Only you can know what changes you could make, if any."

"The one thing I can see is to see another therapist."

He thought he needed to change therapists when he needed to change the way he used therapy. He thought he should quit therapy when he needed to *begin* therapy. In fact, he had engaged in self-destruction for thirty years and called it "psychotherapy."

"You would only be waiting for another therapist to do what no therapist can do. And like you said, you would be helpless waiting for a therapist to rescue you. You've tried that for thirty years. I can't see why you need more evidence for yourself."

"You're not playing devil's advocate?"

"These are facts. You tried being helpless. And it only helped you be better at being helpless. Why pay money to get worse? You already know how to be helpless. You don't need to pay a therapist to do that."

"You say give up."

"You've had a painful life and it's very painful to give up. You have pain and grief about your self-hatred. On the other hand, you want to give up, to have other people take responsibility. I'm pointing out that if you keep wanting people to take responsibility, you will pay a lot of money to get worse."

"Maybe I should exercise the option to try to get better."

"There's always that option."

"If I wanted to get better, I may be able to get better."

Here he offered a hypothetical wish to get better as a substitute for a genuine wish to work in therapy.

"Possibly, but you have to want that. If you want it 1 percent, you'll get a 1 percent result."

"How does one get into a position to want it?"

"You're letting me know you haven't been happy with a 1 percent result. You know it's bullshit, and you don't like bullshit. What can you give to yourself in the time remaining in your life? Therapy is only fifty minutes a week, and the rest of the time there's you. The major factor in therapy is the patient. The therapist is only a tiny percent."

"Hypothetically, you would say I am wasting my time."

"If you're going to do it this way, you already know it's a waste of your time and money. You told me you wasted your time. Doing therapy that way doesn't work. You've been doing it in a way that's guaranteed not to work. That's a lot of money to spend to do therapy in a way that will give you a terrible result."

"Yeah. Well, may I tell my therapist that you said that therapy is a waste of time?"

Again, he thinks therapy is a waste of time when his self-destructive behaviors are destroying his life.

"You can tell him that therapy is a waste of time if you do it this way: 99 percent hopeless and you wait to be rescued. It doesn't make sense."

"You said it's hopeless. You're wasting your money. Why?"

"On the one side, you want to get better. A part of you wants to come out of prison, but another part of you is happy with prison and wants to stay there until you die, justifying prison. As long as you are happy there, you will stay there."

"How do you suggest getting out of prison? How do I change what I want?"

"Why should you change what you want?"

"I don't want to be that way."

"Maybe it's not time to let go of that story. You're holding onto it, so there must be a good reason. Why make yourself want what you don't want?"

"I don't want to want that."

While this is true, he also has spent the past thirty years opposing therapy. We have to help him see that he wants therapy to work and wants to be helpless in therapy. Both are true.

"If we accept you 100 percent today as you are: you've given up, you don't think there's hope. Okay. This is who I'm meeting. Can we accept reality?"

"Maybe I'm in a wheelchair, but you never know if there's a cure for this disease. I may be forever in the wheelchair, but I don't want to lose the chance to get out of the wheelchair."

"We're having to accept that most of you wants to be in the wheelchair."

"Yeah."

"Notice that, accept that, let that be, without having to change it, without having to explain it, without having to push yourself to do anything different."

"I guess you come across hopeless cases."

"Yeah."

"What percentage?"

"Small."

"You just let them go? Wow!"

"I have to accept the facts. If you believe you are hopeless, I have to accept your assessment. You have two parts to your personality: you long for change and you believe you are hopeless and helpless. Both of these forces are alive in you, although hopelessness is the winner. We have to accept that you feel helpless, hopeless, and accept that. These are facts."

"I don't want to accept it. I don't want to accept these facts. I want to fight back when I hear you say this."

"How do you experience this fight back?"

"I don't know. I have some control, and when you say I'm hopeless, I don't believe it. I've had a painful life, but I could change my hope if I wanted to, rather than roll over and die. I would disagree with you. I'm not ready to give up."

"Ready for something else."

"I'm ready to recognize the violence I do to myself, take note of it every time I do it. I don't want to be the way I am. I want to want something. And I don't think I'm 99 percent hopeless." He sat up. "Maybe it's possible."

"Maybe it's possible," I repeated.

"I just need to light the pilot light and get the furnace running."

"The furnace needs to run in you. You have been waiting for the furnace to run in other people. This is a very big insight, and I've rarely heard it said so beautifully. Waiting for someone to be the furnace, and the furnace is you. And all you need is to light the pilot light."

"I think it's lightable. I don't think the furnace is dead."

"No. The furnace can be lit. If you don't light the furnace, then it's dead. Do you want to light this light in you?"

"I want to want to light this light."

"That won't be enough."

"I have to light the pilot light."

"Wanting to want won't be enough," I insisted.

"The furnace may not run at full capacity because it's an old furnace, but it may be semifunctional."

"Even an old furnace can heat up the house."

"It's funny but your bleak picture made me want to fight back. 'He's wrong!'" He started sobbing. Gathering himself, he said, "I do have some control. I can't just go through life with my head down and stay in prison." He sobbed again, stopped, and then shifted. "I think you were playing devil's advocate."

"I was simply saying the truth, and the truth of what you are doing is bleak."

He wept. "It's hard to be positive when you've been negative your whole life."

"It is. And we are noticing it's hard to be positive about yourself. Being negative about yourself has been a slow form of suicide, killing yourself off piece by piece. Now we are learning you want something more."

"I could revert very easily."

"Absolutely. The choice is always there. You can always choose the path of self-hatred."

He paused. "I do have a choice all the time. Get ready to start dying or get ready to start living. Talk is cheap."

"Yes, it is."

"And I'm thinking that you are thinking if I got in touch with my feelings, it would free me up."

Rather than focus on what was in his heart he speculated about what was in my mind. This was how he avoided facing the longings in his own heart.

"Who had that thought?"

"I did."

"Do you want to get in touch with your feelings?"

"Yes."

"Do you feel more freed up?"

"Yes. The fact that I even want to take control . . ."

"This is very important. You want to face your feelings for you. It feels dangerous for you to own that you have a positive wish for yourself. So you attribute it to me. It frightens you to say you want to get freed up. This is very important. You are afraid of the ugliness in you, but you are more afraid of the beauty in yourself, your wish for health, what is good in you, and that's what you try to put in me. You split off the beauty, put it in me, and then regard yourself as ugly. We have to return the healthy wish to you, so everything is in you."

He paused. "I've never thought of it in that way."

"What do you notice feeling as you own that?"

"I'm thinking of a Ray Stevens song: 'Everything is Beautiful.' Probably pie-in-the-sky stuff."

His eyes filled with tears.

"You are very moved."

"I am. I'm sick in my stomach and tired, but I do have the possibility of a different perspective."

"That you could light the furnace. Choosing life rather than roll over and play dead."

He shifted topics by referring to his girlfriend, saying, "I think this girl's a terrible liar."

"That could be, but I wonder: as we reflect on this session, how have you been lying to yourself? The lies you tell yourself are far more dangerous than any lies she could tell you."

"It's an exaggeration to say I'm physically repugnant. That's a slight exaggeration. It's a lie to say I have absolutely no control over anything. It's a lie to say that I have no option but to roll over and play dead and be dead. It's sort of a lie that all people don't care. Some care."

"Who is the person who has cared the least for you?"

He was startled and puzzled. Then I pointed my finger at him.

"Oh. Me. It wouldn't have occurred to me."

"What are the ways you have cared the least for you?"

"By retreating into the shadows. By having such a bad image, but most of all, the constant barrage: You're worthless. You're hopeless. You're not competent. Those are lies I tell myself. As you termed it, being violent to myself. I can grab hold of these concepts and mold them any way I like. If I think I'm not competent, I can try to be competent in some way."

"As we come to a close, what are you feeling?"

"Jon, I feel a lot better. Actually, a lot better. And I started feeling better after you said, 'Let's face it. You're crippled.' And I wanted to fight back." He sobbed again, and then continued, "Maybe I was freed up emotionally and grieving. Maybe when you said, 'You're a hopeless case. There are psychic invalids.' I could fight back if I wished to." He burst into tears again. "I could fight back." Again, he sobbed.

"You could fight back for you, for your life."

"Yeah. I don't know what went wrong in my life."

"You've done a massive wrong to yourself, and you could turn that around. I don't know what wrong was done to you, but you did a massive wrong to yourself and you could change that."

"Every time I have a thought, almost 100 percent of the time, I'll be thinking of the violence to myself and how I wronged myself. Thank you, Jon."

With this breakthrough to grief and guilt over the ways he had sabotaged himself, he began to turn against his self-destructive defenses. He realized that he was in conflict with reality, not me. He hadn't realized that self-sabotage will destroy any therapy, turning it into bullshit.

He saw his miserable life but not how he created it. He thought others didn't care about him when *he* didn't care about himself. He believed others lied to him when he lied to himself. He discovered that he was greater than his lies.

You Will Always Be Greater Than Our Understanding

Truth is an ocean; theory, a cup. We don't realize that those we love remain mysterious to us, even after decades together. Our loved ones are people whom we are always coming to know. And beneath our beliefs lies the unknown person, impenetrable to any ideas but embraceable and, thus, "feelable." Every person will always be greater than the theories in our heads.

We no longer stand over others in a kind of superior "overstanding." We stand under a larger reality, a position that Heidegger reminded us is true understanding.[6] Perhaps it is not so much that we see more deeply into others, but that we see more deeply from within ourselves, from that space in which knowledge arises.

To meet means walking in another person's shoes, encountering someone who is us, because nothing human is alien to us, and not us, because every person is unique. Every person is the center of the universe. We are too. There are many centers.[7]

Relating reaches to the essence of the person under the conditioning. We open ourselves to the person who tries to reach us and whom we try to reach. Or we ask that person to fit into our preconceptions. Yet experience shows us that people were not put on earth to confirm our theories but to contradict them. If we try to fit people into our beliefs, we will never find their essence. As long as we love our images, we will never savor the surprise of meeting the person behind them.

We can imprison people in their histories and in our demands. Then their essence becomes the hand stroking our forehead, waiting for us to awaken from our self-induced coma. If we are fortunate, differences with others rouse us. Opening our eyes, we discern others little by little, and attempt to know them completely. Yet as Heraclitus said, we "cannot discover the bounds of the soul although you pace its every road: so deep is its foundation."[8] Every person is unknowable.

Each of us is a mysterious awareness without space, location, memory, or desire—a silent openness. Theory, however wonderful, is merely a finger pointing toward us.

Given the choice of embracing people or our ideas about them, we must always choose people. Then our thinking will expand to accommodate what is. Are we knowable? No, but we are embraceable. This is what we live in: the embrace.

Epilogue

I can still picture the breeze blowing through the window, curtains swaying, cords hanging, the windowsill gnawed at by tiny teeth. I hear the voices and screams of the past. This window of death is also a portal to life. Each of us is a window through which the truth blows, and every gust of wind is another death. This openness, this yes-ness: the surrender to what is. Do I believe in the awareness that is the embrace? Maybe the day my brother died I heard the song of the wind within. I learned that awareness is not what we do, but who we are. Each of us is a window of awareness, the emptiness in which the truth is revealed. We live in and as the mystery. We are the embrace.

Acknowledgments

I would like to thank those who read and critiqued previous drafts of this book: Zahra Akbarzadeh, Jeremy Bartz, Isabella Bates, Steve Bates, Diane Byster, Linda Campbell, Tim Campbell, Terry DiNuzzo, Allan Gold, Kathleen Golding, Maury Joseph, Binnie Krystal-Anderson, John Lagerquist, Cindy Leavitt, Judy Maris, Tobias Nordqvist, Peter Reder, Maggie Silberstein, Joseph Sokal, Alvin Stenzel, and, especially, Linda Gilbert, without whom this book could not have become what it is. Tony Rousmaniere deserves thanks for suggesting I write this book. And thanks are due Mary Holmes for providing a wonderful place to write. I would also like to thank Peter Fenner for our conversations, the light from which shines throughout the book. Needless to say, any flaws or errors in the book are mine alone. I would also like to thank my previous therapists, supervisors, patients, and teachers whose examples have been an ever-present inspiration to me in my life and work. And, finally, I must express my deepest gratitude to the person who taught me the real meaning of embrace, my wife, Kath.

Notes

Chapter I

1. Sigmund Freud to C. J. Jung, 1906, in *The Freud/Jung Letters* (Princeton, NJ: Princeton University Press, 1994). "Psychoanalysis Is in Essence a Cure through Love."

2. Jeff Foster, *Falling in Love with Where You Are* (New York: Non-Duality Press, 2013).

3. Edwin Shneidman, a prominent researcher of suicide and its causes, proposed that suicide is an attempt to get relief from unbearable psychic pain, what he called "psychache." Edwin Shneidman, *Suicide as Psychache* (New York: Jason Aronson, 1995).

4. I am indebted to the psychoanalyst Edmund Bergler for this phrase in his book *The Superego* (New York: Grune and Stratton, 1952).

5. Wilfred R. Bion, *Seven Servants* (New York: Jason Aronson, 1970).

Chapter 2

1. Byron Katie, *Loving What Is: Four Questions That Can Change Your Life* (New York: Three Rivers Press, 2003).

2. Interestingly, although Freud is well known for having proposed that the patient "say what comes to mind," many therapists do not realize that in 1923 Freud wrote one of his major papers in which he pointed out that patients cannot do this. In fact, they spend most of their time talking *away* from what is important. This led to a major shift in his work: focusing on defenses—the lies we tell ourselves to avoid the pain in our lives.

3. Donald Meltzer, *Studies in Extended Metapsychology: Clinical Applications of Bion's Ideas* (London: Karnac Press, 2009).

4. John Bowlby, *Attachment and Loss,* 3 vols. (New York: Basic Books, 1976–1983).

5. For those wondering about the use of the word "soul," I recommend Bruno Bettelheim's book *Freud and Man's Soul.* Bettelheim describes how Freud used the word "soul" to refer to the depths of the human person, who we are under the words, what is unknown and yet to be known. In fact, the word "psychoanalysis" does not exist in Freud's work. The term he used was *Seeleanalyse*, analysis of the soul.

6. Personal communication from Cindy Leavitt.

7. Every person interested in hope should read Ernst Bloch's *The Principle of Hope.* For what do we do but help people see the hopeless path and find the hopeful one? In addition, see the epilogue of Erich Fromm's *Anatomy of Human Destructiveness* for his beautiful discussion of the difference between optimism as alienated hope and genuine hope based on a sober appraisal of reality.

8. Dag Hammarskjold, *Markings* (New York: Alfred Knopf, 1964).

Chapter 3

1. Plato's *Protagoras* dialogue: Hippocrates: *"And what, Socrates, is the food of the soul?"* Socrates: *"Surely, I said, knowledge is the food of the soul."*
2. Lucie Brock-Broido, *Stay, Illusion: Poems* (New York: Knopf, 2013).
3. John Welwood first coined this term to describe the misuse of spiritual practices to avoid psychological problems.
4. Simone Weil, *Gravity and Grace* (New York: Routledge, 2002).
5. The ancient Roman playwright Terentius.
6. Harry Stack Sullivan was the founder of the interpersonal school of psychiatry.
7. Tertullian is considered the father of Latin Christianity in ancient Rome.
8. Leonard Shengold, *Soul Murder: The Effects of Childhood Abuse and Deprivation* (New York: Ballantine Books, 1991). The psychoanalyst Leonard Shengold explores the ways children's souls are murdered through physical and emotional abuse.
9. Melanie Klein, *Envy and Gratitude and Other Works 1946–1963* (New York: Delacorte Press, 1973).
10. Sigmund Freud, "Remembering, Repeating and Working Through (Further Recommendations in the Technique of Psychoanalysis II)" (1914), in *The Standard Edition of the Complete Psychological Works of Sigmund Freud* (London: Vintage Books, 2001), 12:145–156.

11. John Fiscalini, *Coparticipant Psychoanalysis: Toward a New Theory of Clinical Inquiry* (New York: Columbia University, 2012).

12. Thomas Aquinas, *Summa Theologica* (New York: Christian Classics, 1981).

13. Donald Winnicott, *Maturational Processes and the Facilitating Environment: Studies in the Theory of Emotional Development* (London: Karnac Books, 1966).

14. Herbert Rosenfeld, *Impasse and Interpretation: Therapeutic and Anti-therapeutic Factors in the Treatment of Psychotic, Borderline, and Neurotic Patients* (New York: Routledge, 1987). Rosenfeld discusses the "lavatoric transference," the relationship by which the patient devalues the therapist to avoid envying what the therapist can offer to the patient and what the patient cannot offer herself. French psychoanalysts such as André Green have described this same pattern of devaluation as "fecalization."

15. Theodore L. Dorpat, *Gaslighting, the Double Whammy, Interrogation, and Other Methods of Covert Control in Psychotherapy and Analysis* (New York: Jason Aronson, 1966).

16. Bruno Bettelheim, *Love Is Not Enough* (New York: Free Press, 1950).

17. Aaron Beck, *Love Is Never Enough* (New York: Harper Perennial, 1989).

Chapter 4

1. The tale of the salt doll is known in many nondual traditions such as Buddhism and Hinduism and was used by Ramana Maharshi, among other notable teachers.

2. From the poem, "Im Abendrot," by Joseph Freiherr von Eichendorff, used in Richard Strauss's *Four Last Songs*.

Chapter 5

1. Simone Weil, *Gravity and Grace*.
2. Johann Wolfgang von Goethe, *Scientific Studies* (New York: Suhrkamp, 1988).
3. Goethe. Quoted in Iain MacGilchrist, *The Master and His Emissary: The Divided Brain and the Making of the Western World* (New Haven, CT: Yale University Press, 2012), 36.
4. Wilfred Bion was known as a mystical psychoanalyst in the Kleinian tradition who proposed that we not only have drives of aggression and love but also an instinct to know the truth: epistemophilia.
5. Erich Fromm, *Escape from Freedom* (New York: Holt, 1941).
6. Martin Heidegger, *Zollikon Seminars: Protocols— Conversations—Letters* (Evanston, IL: Northwestern University Press, 2001).
7. Karl Rahner was a noted twentieth-century theologian. This quote is drawn from his book *Spirit in the World* (London: Bloomsbury Press, 1994). For Rahner, all knowledge about a person is knowledge about the being of the world. And whatever conceptual knowledge of the world we have has a horizon, beyond which lies the nonconceptual preknowledge of our being, the ground of all knowing.
8. John Keats, *The Complete Poetical Works and Letters of John Keats,* Cambridge Edition (New York: Houghton Mifflin, 1899).
9. John Fiscalini, *Co-participant Psychoanalysis*.

10. Simone Weil, *Gravity and Grace.*

11. Jose Saramago, from his novel *Blindness* (New York: Harvest Books, 1999).

12. Jean Klein, *Transmission of the Flame* (London: Third Millennium Books, 1994).

Chapter 6

1. Dietrich von Hildebrand, *The Nature of Love* (New York: St. Augustine's Press, 2009). Many of the ideas for this piece were drawn from von Hildebrand.

2. Robert Wolfe, *Living Nonduality: Enlightenment Teachings of Self-Realization* (Ojai, CA: Karina Library, 2014), 235.

3. Based on a Hindu parable that can be found on many sites. For example: www.awakin.org/read/view.php?tid=958.

4. Emily Dickinson, *The Complete Poems of Emily Dickinson* (New York: Back Bay Books, 1976).

5. Many of the ideas I developed in this chapter I borrowed from Peter Wilberg, *The Therapist as Listener: Martin Heidegger and the Missing Dimension of Counseling and Psychotherapy Training* (Eastbourne, UK: New Gnosis, 2004).

6. Martin Heidegger, *Being and Time* (New York: Harper, 2008).

7. Nicolas Berdyaev, *Freedom and Slavery* (New York: Scribner, 1944).

8. Heraclitus, a pre-Socratic Greek philosopher.

About the Author

From the age of six years old, Jon Frederickson grew up working in his father's blacksmith shop in Clear Lake, Iowa. There he worked with his father at the forge and welder, fixing farm implements, and creating wrought iron railings. Although his parents hoped he would take over the shop one day, a music teacher convinced them that Jon had the talent to become a musician and should go on to college. He graduated from college and became a professional musician, playing the French horn. After having received the help of a therapist, he decided to become one. While performing music at night, he went to graduate school during the day and became a social worker and psychotherapist. He worked at a mental health clinic, a counseling center, and later entered private practice.

To further his training, he applied to enter a psychoanalytic institute. But he was informed that they were not sure he was analyzable, due to the traumas in his childhood. He was surprised that he was being evaluated in terms of what had been done to him in the past, not what he had done with his past. He realized how important it is that no person be viewed in terms of what is impersonal, what has been done to us. Instead, we should be judged on what is personal, what we were able to do with the cards we were dealt. He had a new appreciation for the acts of will by which we create ourselves and give meaning to our lives. And this experience gave him new appreciation for the role of hope in life and therapy.

As a faculty member of the Washington School of Psychiatry, he has taught psychiatrists, psychologists, and social workers. Currently, he teaches mental health professionals around the world, showing videotapes of his own work. His life ambition has been to teach therapy as well as his father taught blacksmithing and his music teachers taught the French horn.

Before writing this book for the general public, he authored two books and over thirty articles on psychotherapy. His previous book for therapists was the award winning, *Co-Creating Change: Effective Dynamic Therapy Techniques.*

Jon would love to hear from you. Let him know if these insights and personal stories were helpful. If you have stories and insights that would be helpful to others, Jon would appreciate hearing what you learned so he can share it with others.

You can contact Jon at:

Facebook: https://www.facebook.com/AuthorJonFrederickson.75/

Website: http://www.istdpinstitute.com